Contents

KT-562-678

FACT 1
NERVE SIGNALS TRAVEL FASTER THAN A TRAIN

Your nervous system is a network that carries messages around your body. A signal can travel from your foot to your brain in around 0.02 seconds. That equals 300 km/hour (186 mph), faster than a high-speed bullet train.

THE SPINAL CORD RUNS FROM THE BRAIN DOWN THE BACK. IT IS PROTECTED BY THE VERTEBRAE.

To the brain

Sensory nerves carry messages from your eyes, nose, ears, mouth, and skin. These messages are passed to the Central Nervous System (CNS) which is made up of your brain and spinal cord. The CNS sends messages back through motor nerves, to make your muscles move.

THE HUMAN BODY IS AWESOME!

101 INCREDIBLE THINGS EVERY KID SHOULD KNOW

LISA REGAN

ARCTURUS

ARCTURUS

This edition published in 2017 by Arcturus Publishing Limited
26/27 Bickels Yard, 151–153 Bermondsey Street,
London SE1 3HA

ISBN: 978-1-78428-787-0
CH005647NT
Supplier 26, Date 0617, Print run 6027

Printed in China

Reflex actions

The CNS processes the information it receives from the body and reacts to help you move, stay safe, think, and plan ahead. Some reflexes (such as snatching your hand away from something hot) are controlled directly by the spinal cord, and not by the brain.

Sending signals

Nerves control your body in different ways. As you skate along a path, nerves guide your muscles to make the correct movements to push you along, control your speed, and keep your balance. If a dog runs in front of you, your eyes feed the new information to your brain, which sends electrical impulses to your muscles to make adjustments and stop you having a canine crash!

The spinal cord is about the thickness of a stick of celery.

YOUR LONGEST NERVE IS CALLED THE SCIATIC NERVE, AND IT RUNS FROM THE BASE OF THE SPINE TO THE TOES.

Keeping control

Not all messages to your muscles are voluntary. Some of them happen automatically the whole time. They control your heart rate, breathing, digestion, and many other functions in the body. There are two types of automatic nerve function and they affect the body in opposite ways. The sympathetic nervous system prepares the body for action, sending blood flow to muscles and the lungs. The parasympathetic nervous system slows things down to allow you to rest and recover.

YOUR BRAIN IS CROSS-WIRED!

The human brain consists of two halves. Somewhat bizarrely, the left side of the brain controls the functions on the right side of your body, and vice versa. If you wave your left hand, it's the right side of your brain controlling it.

FACT 3

Your brain makes up only 2 percent of your body weight.

On the outside

The brain looks wrinkled on the outside; this is a covering called the cerebral cortex. It is full of brain cells and can be divided into areas with different special tasks. The cerebral cortex is the biggest part of the human brain and is where your memory lives. It also creates your thoughts and controls your voluntary movements.

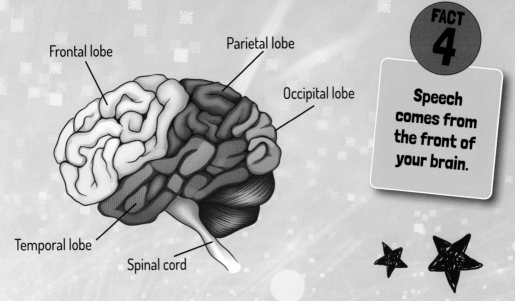

Frontal lobe

Parietal lobe

Occipital lobe

Temporal lobe

Spinal cord

FACT

4

Speech comes from the front of your brain.

Brainy bits

The cerebral cortex has four parts called lobes. Each is responsible for dealing with different types of information. The frontal lobe is where decisions are made, where your personality shapes up, and where all your smart thinking (honestly!) happens. The other three handle sensory input: visual in the occipital lobe, listening and understanding in the temporal lobe, and touch, temperature, and taste in the parietal lobe.

Accidents happen

Scientists learn a lot about the brain by studying when things go wrong. Brain damage, from an injury or an illness, can change a person's personality or affect their ability to speak, walk, or remember things. A stroke (where the blood supply to part of the brain is cut off) on the left side may leave the patient unable to move their right arm or the right side of their face.

I'll just use MY brain to study THIS brain...

THE BRAIN IS A GREEDY ORGAN

The things you eat are used to fuel your body. Food and drink are converted into energy that drives your muscles and keeps your vital organs working. The brain uses up to one fifth of this energy, which is more than any other organ.

Many messages

The neurons (nerve cells) inside your brain are tiny but busy. There are an estimated 100 billion of them firing signals at around 200 times per second. That takes a lot of energy. A neuron looks like a crazy sea creature. A message is sent from the head, down the body, and across to the wavy tentacles of the next neuron. These "tentacles" are called dendrites and can be connected to thousands of other neurons.

neuron

THE BRAIN ALSO USES A HIGH PROPORTION OF THE OXYGEN YOU TAKE ON BOARD: ABOUT ONE QUARTER.

Watermelon is high in vitamin B6, a brain booster.

Brain food

So, your brain is greedy. What can you feed it with? There are suggested foods that are good for your brain's development. Vitamin E (found in seeds and nuts) protects nerve cells. Omega-3 (found in oily fish such as salmon) helps neurons function. Wholegrains help you keep your concentration, and blueberries are said to help your memory. Yummy!

Mental workout

If you're an active person, your muscles will use more energy, and so will your brain. Simply catching a ball requires your brain to work hard: judging where the ball will be, moving your arms, opening and closing your fingers, controlling your balance, changing direction, jumping and landing—all of these increase the brain's energy consumption.

Born again

Many of the body's cells have a short lifespan. They live for days or weeks and then die off and are replaced with new ones. Brain cells, however, don't do that. Why not? Most likely because brain cells store information such as skills, facts, and memories. If you took neurons away, you would lose that information, and have to start again with the new, "blank" cells.

FACT 6 — PLANE TRAVEL CAN MAKE YOU FORGETFUL!

Flying halfway around the world upsets your body clock and disrupts your sleep patterns. Now, scientists think that frequent long-haul flights, for business people and flight attendants, might have long-term effects on the memory.

Making memories

Memories start life in a small part of the brain called the hippocampus. It stores facts and knowledge about how to do things, whether you're trying to remember all the countries of the world, or how to play guitar. Scientists have found that jet lag decreases nerve development in this important area.

FACT 7

Songs are stored in a different part of the brain from other memories.

Must board the 10:15 flight to the Land of Nod...

The long and short of it

Newly formed memories can be kept for a brief time as short-term memories (such as when you are told a phone number), or as long-term memories. These are transferred from the hippocampus to other areas of the brain, for storage. About half of your knowledge and memories arrive through your eyes—something you read, a room full of people, an event you watched. Others are introduced via your other senses.

Writing as you read will help you store more information.

FACT 8

Short-term memories last for only 20–30 seconds, then are committed to long-term memory or lost.

Use it or lose it

Can your brain become so full that you can't store any more information? Put simply—no. You have too much brain space to use it all up! However, constantly accessing the info helps to keep it fresh, so it is harder to remember facts that you haven't used in a long time. Diseases such as Alzheimer's attack the hippocampus and damage short-term memory making, so patients can't remember where they put things, or what they did an hour ago.

Sing along

Repeated exposure to information makes your memory of it stronger. That's why practice is so important and reading your notes over and over again will help you in a test. It is also one of the reasons why you remember song lyrics from years ago. You probably heard them hundreds of times, and if you sang along, that would help to strengthen the memories, too.

YOU HAVE MORE THAN FIVE SENSES

Centuries ago, the great thinker Aristotle wrote about the "five" human senses. Over time, we have learned there are many more ways that our body knows what is happening, both inside and out.

FACT 10

Scientists used to think areas on the tongue identified different tastes. Now we know our taste buds can distinguish all the tastes in all areas.

Extra sensory

Aristotle didn't necessarily think we have only five senses; it was just how he split his writing into chapters. Yet even now, it is commonly said that we have five main senses: sight, hearing, taste, smell, and touch. Senses are where the nerves in certain organs (eyes, ears, mouth, nose, and skin) pass messages to our brain about what we are experiencing. However, the human body is so complex that there are other senses to consider, such as temperature, balance, pain, and our inner state (whether we're hungry, thirsty, or need the bathroom).

RECEPTORS IN THE STOMACH LET US KNOW WHEN WE ARE FULL AND SHOULD STOP EATING.

I am a master of the sixth sense... and the seventh... and the eighth...

It's complicated

Experts don't agree on exactly how many senses there are, but they do agree there are more than five. For example, sight can be divided into two senses, as our eyes have rods (for seeing shapes and movement in low light) and cones (for telling red from blue in broad daylight). Our ears allow us to hear sounds, but also have balance sensors, which pass on information about changing position.

The sense of balance is in your inner ear and is called equilibrioception.

FACT 11

The "itch" sense lets our body know that something on our skin needs attention.

Sensitive skin

Our sense of touch comes from our skin, but covers several distinct aspects with their own receptors. Hot, cold, pain, pressure, and whether we have an itch are all senses in their own right, with their own areas of the brain.

Super sense

Our body also has a sense of where its own parts are in relation to each other. This is called proprioception. It is what allows you to put the tips If your index fingers together in front of you even with your eyes closed, or scratch your toe without looking where your hand needs to be. This sense can be trained and improved by juggling or balancing on one leg.

AN EARDRUM IS THE SIZE OF A FINGERNAIL

The flap on the side of your head is only a small part of your ear. Much more goes on inside to help you hear. The eardrum is part of the inner ear, which contains the smallest bones and muscles in your body.

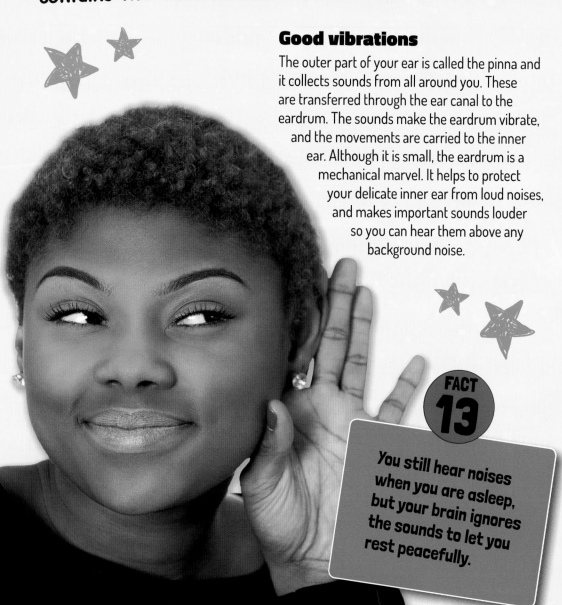

Good vibrations

The outer part of your ear is called the pinna and it collects sounds from all around you. These are transferred through the ear canal to the eardrum. The sounds make the eardrum vibrate, and the movements are carried to the inner ear. Although it is small, the eardrum is a mechanical marvel. It helps to protect your delicate inner ear from loud noises, and makes important sounds louder so you can hear them above any background noise.

FACT
13

You still hear noises when you are asleep, but your brain ignores the sounds to let you rest peacefully.

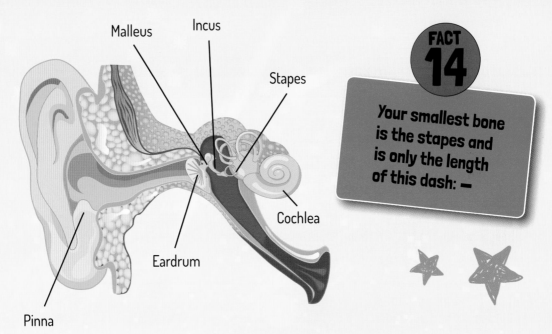

Malleus

Incus

Stapes

Cochlea

Eardrum

Pinna

FACT
14

Your smallest bone is the stapes and is only the length of this dash: —

Highs and lows

Sounds are measured in hertz (Hz): the number of vibrations per second. Humans, on average, can hear a range of sounds between 20Hz and 20,000Hz. Dogs can hear much higher pitched noises, up to around 45,000Hz. Despite their large ears, an elephant can only hear between 16Hz and 12,000Hz.

Can you repeat that?

Hearing problems can be present at birth, or can develop later in life. The delicate parts of the ear are easily damaged by infections, injuries, or loud noises. Our hearing often grows worse as we get older. A hearing aid can be fitted behind the ear or deeper inside to make sounds louder and easier to hear.

On the inside

The inner ear contains three tiny bones (the malleus, incus, and stapes). When the eardrum vibrates, it makes these bones move, which amplifies (makes bigger) the vibrations. The vibrations are passed on to the cochlea, which is the shape of a snail shell and is lined with tiny hairs. Movement in these hairs creates nerve signals that the brain can understand as sounds.

Sign language helps people to communicate without hearing.

15

YOUR EYES SEE UPSIDE DOWN

When you look around you, light is reflected from the things you see. The light enters your eye and creates an image on the back of your eyeball. This image is upside down until your brain does clever things to flip it the right way up.

PEOPLE WITH LONG EYEBALLS ARE SHORT-SIGHTED: THEY CAN'T SEE CLOSE UP VERY WELL.

Trick of the light

The surface at the back of your eye is called the retina and contains light-sensitive cells. These send messages to your brain. The messages are upside down, because they enter your eye through a lens. This lens changes shape to focus on things at different distances. It refracts (bends) the light, making it flip upside down in the process.

Double vision

Light enters your eye through the black hole in the middle (the pupil). The hole grows bigger to let in more light, or shrinks if it is too bright outside. This growth is controlled by tiny muscles in the iris. You receive slightly different signals from each of your eyes, which the brain combines to give a 3-D image and helps you judge the distance away from an object.

YOUR PUPILS GET SMALLER WHEN YOU ARE BORED!

Creatures with eyes at the sides can't judge distance as well as humans.

Seeing stars

Your retina has two types of light sensor: cones and rods. Cones work best in full daylight, allowing you to tell the difference between red, blue, and green. Rods work well in low light, outlining the shape of what you see. You will see distant stars more clearly by gazing slightly to the side. This is because you're using the rods, which are at the outer edge of your retina.

Fast tracking

The white of your eyes is called the sclera. It is a tough, protective coating and has muscles attached to it, to move your eyeballs around. When you watch a moving object—such as a tennis ball—your eyes and head track the movement, but your brain also predicts where the ball is going to be, to make up for the split-second delay in receiving the message from the nerves. That's fast!

YOU CAN SMELL BETTER WHEN YOU'RE HUNGRY

Your sense of smell is more acute when your body is looking for food. Your brain sends messages to your nose that increase your sensitivity to smells, so you are more likely to be successful hunting down a meal.

Good enough to eat

Food smells play an important part in what we eat. Have you ever walked past a restaurant and been tempted to eat, purely because it smells so delicious? Long before fast food and roast dinners, however, smell helped our ancestors decide what was safe to eat. Rotting foods give off bad smells that warn against eating them. Sweet foods, such as ripe fruit, smell a certain way so we know they will give us an instant energy boost.

THE SENSE OF SMELL IS MUCH MORE SENSITIVE THAN TASTE.

Dolphins can't smell anything, even stinky fish!

The science of scent

When we smell something, our nose picks up molecules from the air. This can be hot chocolate wafting across the room, or smoke from a distant fire that could signal danger. Sensory cells send electrical impulses to a part of the brain called the olfactory bulb. These are translated into messages about what we can smell. Intriguingly, dolphins and killer whales don't have this part in their brain, so scientists think they have no sense of smell!

Smells tasty!

The sense of smell is strongly linked with the sense of taste. You may have noticed that you lose your appetite if you have a blocked nose. Chewing food releases aromas from the back of the mouth up to the nasal chamber, the space behind the nose. This gives more information to the brain and makes food taste better.

Super sensitive

Some noses are more sensitive than others. It may be that they react more to allergens such as pollen or dust. Other noses can detect many more different smells than the average nose. This can be a valuable talent, leading to a career in perfumery or as a chef, for example. It's all down to how many smell receptors you have in your nose, and how your brain interprets the messages.

FACT 17

YOU ARE AS FAST AS AN OLYMPIAN!

Not at running, obviously. But certain things in your body work as fast as those in a sprinter's body—for example, the muscles in your eyes. Humans generally have similar reaction times when they are in danger, too.

Ouch!

Your senses help to keep you safe from things around you. For example, you can smell if something is on fire, or your sense of touch will tell you when something is hot. The reaction time if you come into contact with extreme heat, such as a hot serving dish, is around 100 milliseconds. Your brain will tell your muscles to pull your hand away at top speed, whether you're an Olympic sprinter or not.

ATHLETES TRAIN TO REDUCE THEIR REACTION TIME WHEN THEY HEAR THE STARTING PISTOL.

Spiky or smooth?

Skin is the main organ for the sense of touch. Touch sensors pass messages to your brain, informing it what's out there. There are many different types of sensor, picking up sensations such as heat and cold, vibrations and tickles, and whether something is rough or smooth or spiky or slimy or sticky.

Touch tells you the difference between spiky and rough.

YOUR BRAIN FILTERS OUT MESSAGES THAT AREN'T NEEDED, LIKE THE TOUCH OF CLOTHES ON YOUR BODY.

Pain and pleasure

Your skin has more receptors for pain than for the other sensations. Some parts of your body have more sensors than others, making them more sensitive. You have most on your lips, tongue, face, fingers, and soles of your feet, and least on your torso (especially the back), arms, and legs.

Strange sensations

Touch messages are carried to your brain by your nervous system. Sometimes these pathways can be damaged or temporarily blocked. If you lean too heavily on your arm, for instance, it can squash the nerves (and the blood vessels that supply them with oxygen) and make your arm go numb. When the pressure is taken off, blood floods back to the area, the nerves fire back into action, and you get the feeling of pins and needles.

TEAMS THAT BOND THROUGH TOUCH WIN MORE OFTEN THAN TEAMS THAT DON'T TOUCH.

SLEEP CAN MAKE YOU TIRED

Sleep is designed to rest your body, allowing you to grow and boost your energy levels. But for some people, nights are far from relaxing. They scream, shout, punch, and run in their sleep, leaving them exhausted.

LACK OF SLEEP CAN INCREASE YOUR APPETITE AND MAKE YOU OVEREAT.

Not-so-sweet dreams

Sleep disorders can literally be a nightmare. Patients with a condition called REM-Sleep Disorder physically act out their dreams, by running on the spot, yelling, thrashing, and kicking. It can also cause sleepwalking.

Movers and shakers

REM stands for Rapid Eye Movement, where the eyes twitch and move around. The brain stops the rest of the body's muscles during this time, probably to protect us from thrashing around and causing injuries. REM is one of five stages of sleep, and is the period where dreams happen. It usually accounts for up to a quarter of your total sleep time.

Babies need to sleep for up to 17 hours a day.

RELATIVES OF DEAF PEOPLE HAVE SEEN THEM USE SIGN LANGUAGE IN THEIR SLEEP.

Sleep well

Lack of quality sleep may affect your brain and your immune system. It can make you worse at problem solving, reasoning, concentrating, and remembering new information. You are more likely to get ill, and will take longer to recover from a cold. Adults need around eight hours of sleep each night, but younger people tend to need more: between nine and ten hours.

Pass it on

Have you noticed that yawning can be infectious? If you see somebody yawn, it often makes you do the same. It is thought that it is because yawning is designed to keep us awake: it cools down the brain. Our ancient instincts kick in to make us more alert, in case there is danger on the horizon. However, studies show that this phenomenon only affects about 50 percent of people.

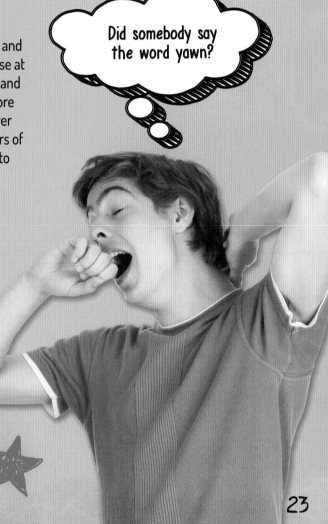

Did somebody say the word yawn?

23

FACT 19
YOU LOSE BONES AS YOU GROW UP

The skeletal system forms a framework that supports your whole body. Without it, you would be floppy, like a rag doll. A newborn baby has more than 300 bones, but some of these join together as the child grows.

Making bones

A baby's bones are mostly made of cartilage. That's the tough but flexible substance that makes up most of your outer ear, underneath the flesh. As a baby grows, a process called ossification takes place. Extra calcium turns the cartilage into bone, becoming hard and strong. Some of the smaller bones fuse, or join, together in the process.

FACT 20
The adult human skeleton is made up of 206 bones.

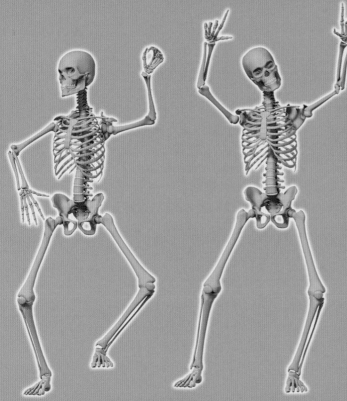

Tough stuff

Your skeleton allows you to stand tall and move around. It also acts as a protective framework around your soft parts, such as your internal organs. The skull is vital for shielding your brain, and the ribs form a cage with your heart, liver, and lungs inside. The spinal cord runs through the middle of a chain of backbones called vertebrae.

Move it!

Of course, your skeleton cannot move around on its own. You need muscles for movement. They are attached to your bones to pull them into place. The bones fit together and bend at joints, such as the ankle and the elbow. Some joints bend in a fixed direction, while others allow a wide range of movement, like the shoulder.

Broken bones

Bones are tough, but they can break (this is called a fracture). Bones can snap or crack or even shatter. Ouch! When this happens, the bone must be set back into position and held there, usually with a plaster cast, until it mends. Your body will make new bone cells and blood vessels to close up the broken part.

FACT 21 Bones make up about one fifth of your total body weight.

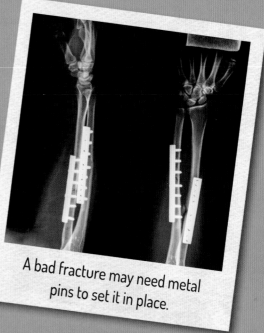

A bad fracture may need metal pins to set it in place.

THE MOTORCYCLE STUNT RIDER EVEL KNIEVEL BROKE MORE THAN 400 BONES DURING HIS CAREER (SOME BONES BROKE MORE THAN ONCE!)

25

YOUR HEAD HAS MORE BONES THAN YOUR HAND

You may think your head contains just a few large bony plates, but it actually has eight skull bones and fourteen more in your face. On the other hand (ha ha), a hand has only nineteen bones inside.

EACH EAR CONTAINS THREE BONES, ADDING ANOTHER SIX TO THE TOTAL.

Head case

An adult human's skull is made up of large plates joined at wavy junctions called sutures. These sutures are flexible when you're a child, to allow the brain to grow inside. It does this at an amazing rate: from one third the size of an adult brain at birth, it more than doubles in the next 90 days. The back of the skull has a hole at the bottom for the spinal cord, which connects to the brain.

Well, that's a handy fact to know!

Face facts

The face is made up of smaller bones. Most of these are arranged in pairs, which is why your face is roughly symmetrical. Only two face bones are "solo" bones: the vomer, which divides your nose cavity in two, and the jawbone. The jawbone, or mandible, forms the lower part of your mouth, and is the only face bone that moves.

Six pairs of bones make the face symmetrical.

YOUR KNUCKLES ARE THE ENDS OF YOUR METACARPAL BONES.

Hands and feet

Let's take a look at your hands and feet. Each finger contains three bones (phalanges), and there are two in your thumb. These are linked to five metacarpals in the palms. Your feet may appear very different, but inside they're much the same, and have 21 bones each. However, if you include your wrist and ankle bones (eight per wrist, five per ankle) in the total, your hands and feet contain over half of the bones in your body.

Best foot forward

Humans walk upright, and so their feet have to be strong to carry their whole body weight. The largest bones in feet are the heel bones, the calcaneus and talus. They are important to help you balance on uneven surfaces. The feet have to be flexible and supple, and contain more than a hundred muscles, tendons, and ligaments. Foot and ankle injuries are common, but broken bones less so.

27

THE FEMUR IS A QUARTER OF YOUR HEIGHT

The longest bone in the human body is the femur, in the thigh. Each leg contains three strong bones to carry your weight as you walk and run. The fourth leg bone is the patella, or kneecap.

FACT 24

The bumpy bits that feel like ankle bones are actually the outer parts of your fibula and tibia.

Long legs

The femur is in the top half of your leg. In most humans, it measures roughly one fourth of your height. Below the knee, you have the tibia and fibula. These are all examples of "long bones"—one of the five types of bone. They are longer than they are wide, with a knobbly bump called the epiphysis at each end. This is made of growth plates where cells multiply to make the bone bigger or longer.

LONG BONES CAN BE SMALL, SUCH AS THE METACARPALS IN YOUR HAND.

All shapes and sizes

Short bones are cube-shaped, such as the ones in your wrists and ankles. They are strong but move less than long bones. Sesamoid bones are small and circular and found within tendons. Your shoulder blade, pelvis, and cranium (skull) are examples of flat bones. These are the ones that offer protection to what's hiding beneath, like a shield or a helmet.

FACT 25

Weight-for-weight, bones are six times stronger than steel.

Crazy bones

The fifth type of bones are those that don't fit into any other category. They are called irregular bones. They include the sacrum and the coccyx (at the base of the spine), the jawbone, and very importantly your vertebrae. These are disk-shaped bones with a hole in the middle to surround and protect the spinal cord.

In and out

Your chest is shaped by a basket of flat bones called the ribs. There are 12 pairs of different sizes, and they are easily broken. Simply sneezing or coughing violently can fracture them. Gaps between the ribs are filled with muscle that expands and contracts as we breathe; it moves 3 to 5 cm (1 to 2 in) with every breath.

Coughing hard can actually fracture a rib.

29

FACT 26 YOUR BONES ARE FILLED WITH GOO!

The bones inside your body are not brittle and dry like the dead ones you see in a museum. They are growing structures made of living tissue and hard minerals. Some contain a gooey substance inside.

Inside a bone

Bones are not solid all the way through. They have different layers. Compact bone is smooth and hard, and is the part you see in a skeleton on display. Living bones have a thin outer layer surrounding this, called the periosteum. Inside the compact bone is a strong, spongy substance called cancellous bone. This protects the "goo," which is a jelly-like substance called bone marrow.

BONES ARE ABOUT ONE-FIFTH WATER.

FACT 27

Your bone marrow produces more than 200 billion red blood cells each day.

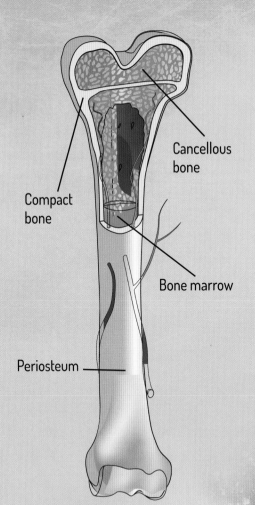

Cancellous bone

Compact bone

Bone marrow

Periosteum

Brilliant bones

The periosteum is important to living bones. It contains nerves and blood vessels to supply nutrients and help bones grow and heal. Compact bone is very dense and strong, to give your body support. Cancellous bone has lots of air inside, so it is lightweight but still strong. It looks a bit like honeycomb and acts like a shock absorber for high impact movements, from running and jumping to skiing and martial arts.

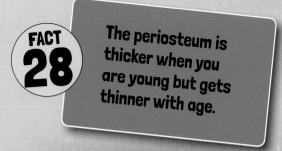

FACT 28

The periosteum is thicker when you are young but gets thinner with age.

Cell factory

Flat bones and long bones have another substance inside. This is bone marrow, and it is where new blood cells are made. When you are born, all your bone marrow is red. As you get older, some is converted to yellow, containing a larger number of fat cells.

Smooth moves

Bones are made of tough stuff. They move and rub together, and would grind themselves down without protection. Your joints are protected by another squashy substance, called cartilage (see page 24). It acts like a cushion, and sometimes has synovial fluid around it to keep the joint "oiled" and moving easily.

YOU SHRINK DURING THE DAY

Don't panic! You don't shrink very much, but you may be shorter at bedtime than when you first wake up. Over the course of the day, gravity takes effect on your spine and it can shrink by around a finger's width.

Help! Is it bedtime yet?

Back to basics

Your spine consists of a long row of vertebrae with disks in between them. These act as shock absorbers for the main bones. They contain a large amount of water and get squashed down as we sit, stand, and move around. At night, fluid shifts back into the disks to expand them again. A tiny amount of squashing in each disk adds up to around 1 cm (½ in) overall.

THE SPINE CONTAINS MORE THAN 120 MUSCLES.

Spinal spring

Your spine forms a natural S-shaped curve, inward at your neck and lower back, and slightly outward in the middle. It acts like a spring to keep you balanced and help you move smoothly without jarring your body. You have seven vertebrae in your neck (the same as most other mammals, from moles to giraffes). The top two are specially designed to allow extra movement, for nodding and shaking and turning your head.

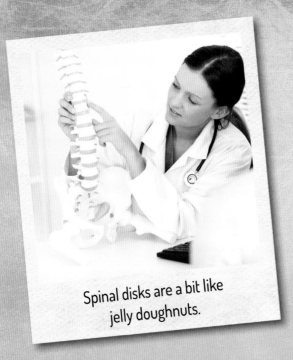

Spinal disks are a bit like jelly doughnuts.

THERE ARE 33 VERTEBRAE BUT ONLY THE TOP 24 ARE MOVABLE.

Bonded bones

The bones in the spine are among those that fuse to give adults fewer bones than babies. A baby has 33 vertebrae, and as it grows, the bottom four fuse to make the coccyx or tailbone, and the five above that bond together to make the back of the pelvis (the sacrum).

Passing through

Each of your vertebrae has a solid section plus an arch-shaped piece. These arches line up on top of each other to form a protective, flexible "tunnel" for the spinal cord to run through. The spinal cord is the widest nerve in the body. It is around 2 cm wide (¾ in) and connects other nerves in the body to the brain.

THE SPINE IS SO FLEXIBLE IT CAN FORM TWO-THIRDS OF A CIRCLE.

CHILDREN ARE BENDIER THAN ADULTS

Flexible tissues called ligaments and tendons link and move your joints. They are slightly stretchy, and some people naturally stretch farther than others. As you get older, you lose flexibility, although daily stretching helps.

And...stre-e-etch

Your muscles and bones work together to allow you to move. But they need the help of other tissues. Ligaments are slightly stretchy cords that fix your bones together at their joints, and hold them safely in place. Tendons are thicker and less elastic, and attach your muscles to your bones. Staying fit keeps these body parts in good shape.

Bend it

Some super-bendy people can move their body into positions that seem impossible to other people. They are said to be double-jointed, but they don't have more joints than anyone else. Their ligaments may have less collagen (a protein that keeps your tissues strong); this trait can run in the family and is known as hypermobility.

Hypermobility allows you to bend further than normal.

THE ACHILLES TENDON AT THE BACK OF THE LEG IS THE THICKEST IN THE BODY.

Loosen up

Special exercises will help your body become more flexible. Yoga is especially good for training the joints and muscles to move more. It is important to stretch and "warm up" before sports and exercise, to loosen and lengthen your muscles, tendons, and ligaments. Jogging for a few minutes will pump blood to your muscles and joints so they are ready to perform without getting injured.

Stop!

Your brain sends nerve signals to the muscles to make them move. Sensors in the tendons send signals back to let the brain know if the muscle is being overstretched. Your body has its own warning system to prevent serious damage. That's why a losing arm wrestler's arm collapses at the end of a bout: the nerves are telling the tendon to stop before injury occurs.

You've overstretched yourself, mister.

EXERCISE CAN MAKE YOU GAIN WEIGHT

Our bodies store extra water when our exercise levels increase, which can lead to an increase in weight. Water is used to help repair small tears to the muscles caused by exercise. It's also stored in the form of glycogen, which gives the body energy.

Building up

Everyone has the same number of muscles, but fit, strong, "muscly" people have built up their muscles through exercise. The more you use muscles, the bigger they grow. Bigger muscles have improved blood flow to supply more energy and oxygen. Eating high-protein foods (such as meat, dairy, fish, eggs, and beans) can also help to make muscles grow larger and stronger.

YOUR MUSCLES MAKE UP AROUND 40 PERCENT OF YOUR TOTAL WEIGHT.

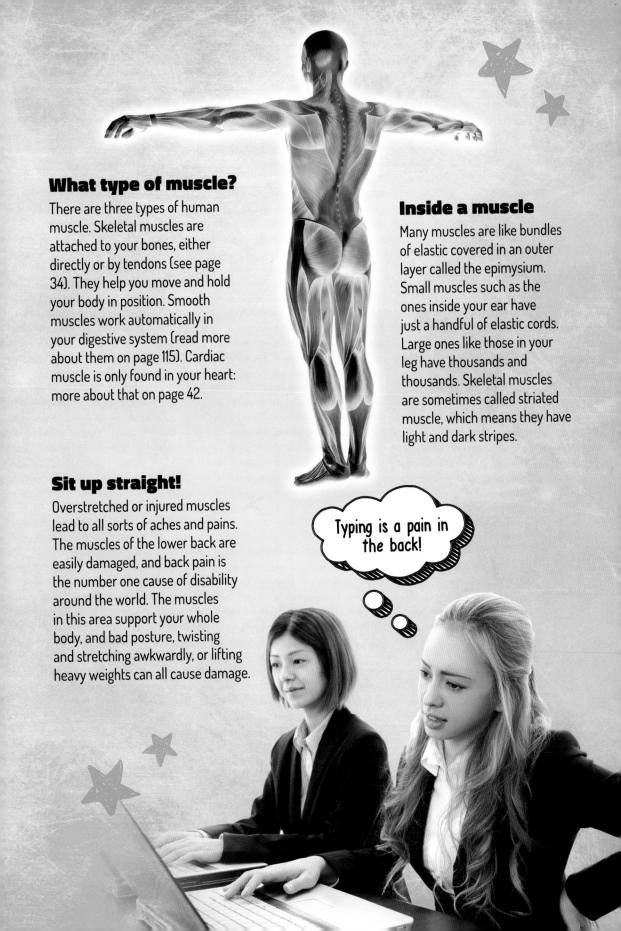

What type of muscle?

There are three types of human muscle. Skeletal muscles are attached to your bones, either directly or by tendons (see page 34). They help you move and hold your body in position. Smooth muscles work automatically in your digestive system (read more about them on page 115). Cardiac muscle is only found in your heart: more about that on page 42.

Inside a muscle

Many muscles are like bundles of elastic covered in an outer layer called the epimysium. Small muscles such as the ones inside your ear have just a handful of elastic cords. Large ones like those in your leg have thousands and thousands. Skeletal muscles are sometimes called striated muscle, which means they have light and dark stripes.

Sit up straight!

Overstretched or injured muscles lead to all sorts of aches and pains. The muscles of the lower back are easily damaged, and back pain is the number one cause of disability around the world. The muscles in this area support your whole body, and bad posture, twisting and stretching awkwardly, or lifting heavy weights can all cause damage.

Typing is a pain in the back!

FACT 32 MUSCLES PULL BUT CANNOT PUSH

Skeletal muscles stretch and contract to move the bone they are attached to. They have to work in pairs (called antagonistic pairs) to pull the bone in opposite directions.

FACT 33 If you could hear below 20Hz you would hear your own muscles moving.

Bend it

The triceps and biceps in your upper arm are examples of antagonistic muscles. As your biceps shortens, it pulls your forearm upward to bend your arm. The triceps underneath relaxes to allow this. To straighten your arm, the triceps pulls in the opposite direction as your biceps relaxes. A muscle can shorten to 85 percent of its resting length, and stretch to 120 percent.

YOUR FINGERS DON'T HAVE MUSCLES. FINGER MOVEMENTS ARE MADE BY MUSCLES IN YOUR PALM AND ARM.

Fast and slow

There are different types of skeletal muscles to achieve different things. Slow-twitch muscles contain lots of blood vessels and are red. They are good for aerobic activities that use oxygen, such as cycling and swimming. Fast-twitch muscles are paler. They produce large amounts of energy in a short time, and don't use oxygen. They are used in anaerobic actions, like sprinting and jumping, or for strength events such as weightlifting.

The long jump uses powerful fast-twitch muscles.

FACT 34

You shiver to make your muscles move, which generates heat to warm you up.

Which are you?

Each of us has a mixture of fast- and slow-twitch within a single muscle. The proportions vary, and play a part in the kind of activities you are best at. So from birth, it's already forecast whether you will excel at stamina events, or be better at more explosive sports (and no, that doesn't mean rifle shooting!).

Warming up

Muscles are stiffer when they are cold, whether it's because of the temperature outside, or because you haven't used them much. It is easier to overstretch and tear a muscle when it is stiff. This is known as straining or pulling a muscle, and can be extremely painful. It can take longer to heal than a fractured bone.

39

FACT 35

YOUR EYES GET A MEGA—WORKOUT EACH DAY

Your eyes have muscles around them and inside them. They move around 100,000 times each day, to focus, control the light, scan for objects, and follow moving things.

YOUR EYES MOVE NEARLY 10,000 TIMES IF YOU READ FOR AN HOUR.

Eye, eye!

The eye muscles are stronger, in proportion to the small size and weight of the eyeball, than any other muscles. Six skeletal muscles hold the eyeball in its socket and move it around so you can look up, down, and sideways. They also cleverly adjust each eye to produce a single image instead of a blurred one.

Fascinating faces

The many muscles in your face are unusual as so many of them are connected only to skin, not bones. They allow you to change your expression, from disgust or fear to happiness or surprise. Muscles also move your bones so that you can bite, chew, swallow, talk, see, and hear.

T-time

One large set of muscles helps you move food around to chew it: those in your tongue. They are also unusual as they are only attached at one end. Four muscles make the tongue change shape (pointing, curling, even rolling and folding it). Four more are attached to the bones of your head, and allow changes in position (poking in and out or moving sideways).

Talking, biting, chewing, and smiling—it's a real workout!

ON AVERAGE, MEN'S TONGUES ARE LONGER THAN WOMEN'S.

Tell me about it

Four muscles around your mouth move your lips for speaking, whistling, and (blush) kissing. However, many additional muscles are needed to talk: around 100! It starts with your diaphragm and core muscles, pushing breath up and out. The breath passes through your vocal cords and is shaped into words by your tongue, lips, cheeks, and jaw.

MUSCLES HAVE A MIND OF THEIR OWN!

If you've ever accidentally bitten your own tongue or cheek, you'll know it hurts. It can happen when your muscles are working for themselves, without you concentrating.

OUCH! How did I bite my own cheek?

Heart of the matter

You can control your skeletal muscles to perform the actions you want. Sometimes, though, your brain makes mistakes, and accidents happen, like biting your cheek. Your body has different types of muscles that work alone all the time to pump your blood, digest food, and help you breathe. Cardiac muscle makes your heart beat without your brain having to think about it. It can work constantly without getting tired.

MUSCLES IN YOUR EYELIDS MAKE YOU BLINK. BABIES ONLY BLINK ONCE OR TWICE A MINUTE!

Can muscles remember?

The term "muscle memory" is often applied to actions that you have done over and over again until they are stored in your long term memory. Your brain knows them so well, it can perform them with very little neural activity. It happens with everyday tasks like walking or washing your hair, and more specialist skills like typing, driving a car, hitting a golf ball, playing piano, or serving in tennis.

Learn the correct swing and it will become second nature.

THE HEART MUSCLE IS STRONG ENOUGH TO PUMP BLOOD 9 M (30 FT) ACROSS THE ROOM!

Feeling twitchy

Muscles can also trigger movements that you don't want to happen. Have you ever felt your eyelid twitching, as if you can't stop winking? That's a muscle contracting over and over, and even doctors aren't sure of the cause. Some people twitch out of habit (known as a tic), making them wink, blink, screw up their face, and even jerk and mutter.

Involuntary muscle

Your body has a third kind of muscle. It is called smooth muscle, and is found in your inner organs such as the bladder, stomach, and intestine. These muscles contract and relax on their own to help your organs do their work. Muscles in the bladder control the urge to pee. Muscles in the digestive system push food on its way; either down, to be digested, or up and back out, if something makes you sick.

FACT 37 SOME PEOPLE HAVE MISSING MUSCLES!

Genetic mutations have led to some people being born without certain muscles, and because they're not really used in our body, they aren't missed—and the mutation is passed on to the next generation.

Now you see it...

There are various parts of the body that aren't missed if they're not there. Touch your thumb tip to your little fingertip and tilt them slightly to your wrist. You should see a long, thin muscle stick out from your wrist. That's your palmaris longus, but it is missing in over 10 percent of people without any negative effects. A leg muscle called the plantaris is also missing in around 10 percent of people.

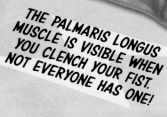

THE PALMARIS LONGUS MUSCLE IS VISIBLE WHEN YOU CLENCH YOUR FIST. NOT EVERYONE HAS ONE!

Needed or not?

The appendix is often given as an example of a vestigial organ. It is a small tube in your digestive system and can be removed if it becomes infected, without the patient missing it. Recent research, however, debates its usefulness. It may no longer be needed for digesting uncooked food, but it probably acts as a store for useful digestive bacteria.

Taking out the appendix is a common and routine operation.

Missing organs

The kidneys generally work in pairs, to filter your blood. However, some people are born with only one, or donate one for surgery, and can live perfectly well without the second one. The liver, too, is amazing. It works really hard to perform many tasks, but if part of it is removed, it can regrow itself from as little as a quarter of its original size!

...now you don't

Parts that were once there but have been lost through time are called vestigial body parts. They include the occipitalis major, a muscle at the back of the head. It moves the scalp, so if you have one, it allows you to wiggle your ears. Human ears have no muscles, whereas dogs and cats have over twelve to allow them to move their ears in all sorts of ways.

FACT 38

YOUR HEART IS THE SIZE OF YOUR FIST

Your heart is a muscle that pumps blood around your body. The blood supplies nutrients and oxygen, and clears away waste products that your body doesn't need.

Special delivery

Your heart and your blood vessels make up your circulatory system. Stretched out in a long line, a person's blood vessels would be about 100,000 km (60,000 miles) long—over twice around the Earth! The heart is tucked behind your ribs, nearly in the middle of your chest, but slightly to the left. It constantly works hard to pump your blood to all your body bits.

IT TAKES ABOUT 45 SECONDS FOR YOUR BLOOD TO MAKE A COMPLETE CIRCUIT.

Fully loaded

Blood carries all sorts of things that your body needs. It delivers nutrients, hormones, antibodies, and helps control your temperature. One drop of blood contains five million red blood cells, half a million platelet cells, 7,000 white blood cells, and a mixture of sugar, salt, vitamins, protein, fat, and water. Red blood cells carry oxygen, while white blood cells fight disease (see page 56).

Waste disposal

Blood also transports waste products so they can be removed from the body. It carries carbon dioxide, which you breathe out. It also takes urea, produced in the liver, to your kidneys for them to turn it into urine. You know how that leaves the body! Lactic acid, created during exercise, is moved to your liver to be broken down.

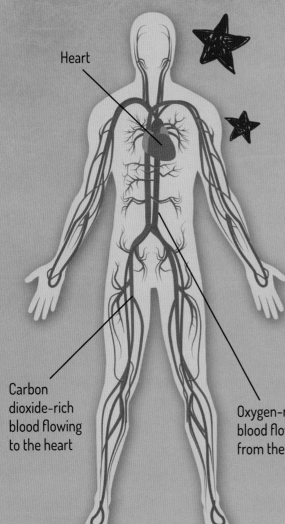

Heart

Carbon dioxide-rich blood flowing to the heart

Oxygen-rich blood flowing from the heart

BLOOD LOOKS BLUE UNDER YOUR SKIN, BUT THAT'S ONLY BECAUSE OF THE WAY LIGHT IS REFLECTED.

Hot blooded

Heat receptors in the blood and the skin send messages to your brain about your body temperature. An area called the hypothalamus reacts if you are too hot or cold. It triggers changes in your muscles and sweat glands to get your body back to a safe temperature.

Sweat evaporates into the air and helps lose body heat.

A HEARTBEAT HAS FOUR PARTS

The heart is actually two pumps next to each other. One half sends oxygen around the body, while the other half goes to the lungs to collect more supplies. Each half beats in and out all the time.

Four phases

A single heartbeat takes less than a second. During that time, the heart relaxes and contracts once in each half. The four phases are: the first diastole, when the blood flows into the right-hand side. The first systole, when the heart contracts so the blood flows out toward the lungs. The second diastole sees blood fill the left-hand side, and in the second systole phase, blood is pumped out to the rest of the body. It all makes the familiar lub-dub, lub-dub of a heartbeat.

EACH HEARTBEAT PUMPS OUT ABOUT A CUPFUL OF BLOOD.

Four parts working together—that's us rowers AND my heart!

One-way traffic

A heart consists of four chambers. The right atrium and left atrium are at the top. Two ventricles sit below these. They are linked by special one-way valves that stop blood flowing freely backward and forward. Valves around the rest of your body ensure that blood keeps moving in the right direction. They help prevent gravity taking effect so all your blood doesn't end up in your feet!

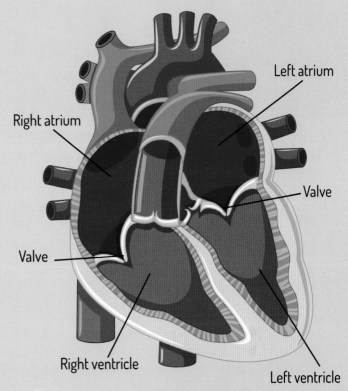

Left atrium

Right atrium

Valve

Valve

Right ventricle

Left ventricle

THE SOUND OF THE VALVES OPENING AND CLOSING IS YOUR HEARTBEAT.

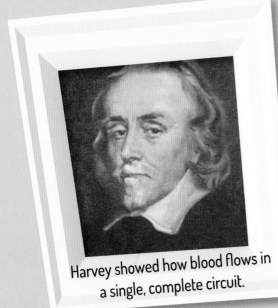

Harvey showed how blood flows in a single, complete circuit.

Oxygen boost

The blood that arrives in your right atrium is dark red. It has little oxygen as your body has used it up. The heart sends it to the lungs for a fresh supply. Once the blood has been reoxygenated, it arrives in the left atrium and is bright red, ready to pump around your whole body again.

Making history

No one really understood blood's journey around the body before the 1600s. In 1618, a doctor named William Harvey became the royal physician: the official doctor of the king of England. He studied animals to find out about blood. In 1628 he published a groundbreaking book, *On the Motion of the Heart and Blood*, explaining how the heart moved blood around the body in a circular fashion.

Blood is carried around the body in thin, stretchy tubes called blood vessels. There are three types, each performing a different task. They are arteries, veins, and tiny capillaries.

Getting around

The bright red blood that is full of oxygen travels away from your heart in arteries. It comes back to the heart in veins. Arteries need to have thicker walls and layers of muscle, as the blood flowing along them is under high pressure after being pumped by the heart. Capillaries branch off from the arteries to carry food and oxygen to the cells that use them.

FACT 41 The cornea at the front of the eye has no blood supply; it gets its oxygen from the air.

CAPILLARIES ARE TINY—EVEN THE LARGEST IS THINNER THAN A HAIR.

Back again

Each of your major organs has its own artery and vein to get their supplies. At any moment in time, about three-quarters of your blood is in the veins, on the way back to the heart. Roughly one-fifth is in your arteries, and only a small amount (one-twentieth) is in the capillaries.

FACT 42

Newborn babies have around a cupful of blood, while adults have up to 5.5 l (1.5 gallons).

Major highway

The largest artery in the body is the aorta. It is as thick as your thumb, and shaped like a walking stick. It starts at the top of your heart then curves over and downward, through the chest, past the diaphragm, and down in front of your spine. Then it divides in two to go down each leg. Smaller arteries branch off it, like roads off a busy highway.

Blood for your heart

Although the heart is full of blood, it cannot use it as its own supply. The heart pumps so fast and at such high pressure that it would burst any capillaries inside it. Instead, it has its own special coronary arteries that wrap around the outside to send nutrients to the heart itself. Blocked arteries are a common cause of heart attacks.

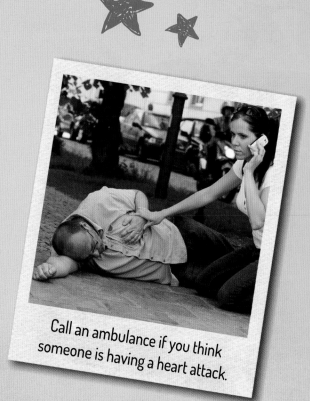

Call an ambulance if you think someone is having a heart attack.

ENERGY DRINKS CAN BE DANGEROUS

Exercise makes your heart beat faster, and so do certain emotions, like surprise, fear, and anger. Caffeine has the same effect, and some energy drinks can make your heart beat dangerously fast.

FACT 45

Your heart beats 100,000 times a day, which is around 30 million heartbeats each year.

Danger drinks

Caffeine is found in coffee, tea, and cola. It stimulates the system and speeds up the heart rate and flow of blood around the body. Energy drinks contain high levels of caffeine and can be dangerous if you drink them too often. Studies have shown they raise the heart rate by eight percent, and the effects can take hours to wear off.

ENERGY DRINKS CAN CAUSE PALPITATIONS—THE FEELING THAT YOUR HEART IS FLUTTERING OR POUNDING.

Back again

Each of your major organs has its own artery and vein to get their supplies. At any moment in time, about three-quarters of your blood is in the veins, on the way back to the heart. Roughly one-fifth is in your arteries, and only a small amount (one-twentieth) is in the capillaries.

FACT 42

Newborn babies have around a cupful of blood, while adults have up to 5.5 l (1.5 gallons).

Major highway

The largest artery in the body is the aorta. It is as thick as your thumb, and shaped like a walking stick. It starts at the top of your heart then curves over and downward, through the chest, past the diaphragm, and down in front of your spine. Then it divides in two to go down each leg. Smaller arteries branch off it, like roads off a busy highway.

Blood for your heart

Although the heart is full of blood, it cannot use it as its own supply. The heart pumps so fast and at such high pressure that it would burst any capillaries inside it. Instead, it has its own special coronary arteries that wrap around the outside to send nutrients to the heart itself. Blocked arteries are a common cause of heart attacks.

Call an ambulance if you think someone is having a heart attack.

51

BABIES BREATHE FOUR TIMES FASTER YOU

As you sit reading this book, you are probably breathing around 15 times per minute. Newborn babies take lots more breaths, as many as 60 per minute!

ADULTS CANNOT BREATHE AND SWALLOW AT THE SAME TIME, BUT BABIES CAN!

Baby breaths

You breathe in order to get oxygen and remove carbon dioxide. At rest, you breathe slowly, but if you exercise, or get scared or excited, you breathe faster to take in more oxygen and expel more waste. Babies breathe extremely quickly, but settle into slower breathing as their lungs and bodies grow.

Breathing's just one of my many skills.

Faster and faster

During exercise, your heart begins to beat more quickly, too, to deliver more fuel to your muscles and remove waste faster. A healthy adult heart beats between 60 and 80 times a minute, but rises when the body is working hard (and beats at between 150 to 200 times a minute). Yet again, a baby's heart beats a lot faster, even at rest: about 130 bpm (beats per minute).

High-energy sports such as squash make your heart pound!

BEING THIRSTY CAN AFFECT YOUR HEART RATE. DRINK PLENTY OF WATER!

Hole in the heart

Sometimes, a baby is born with a heart problem. One of the most common is the "hole in the heart." The wall dividing the two sides of the heart (called the septum) may have a tiny opening that allows blood to seep through. It can be fixed with surgery, or may even close up by itself.

Before birth

The heart develops very early in an unborn baby. It starts beating about three weeks after the baby was conceived. At first it beats around 85 times per minute, but rises to a speedy 175 bpm before settling into a pattern between 120–160 bpm until birth. An ultrasound scan allows medics to check that a baby's heart is beating properly.

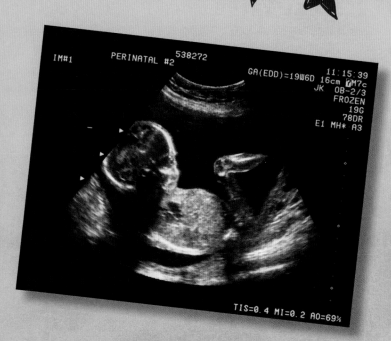

FACT 44
ENERGY DRINKS CAN BE DANGEROUS

Exercise makes your heart beat faster, and so do certain emotions, like surprise, fear, and anger. Caffeine has the same effect, and some energy drinks can make your heart beat dangerously fast.

FACT 45

Your heart beats 100,000 times a day, which is around 30 million heartbeats each year.

Danger drinks

Caffeine is found in coffee, tea, and cola. It stimulates the system and speeds up the heart rate and flow of blood around the body. Energy drinks contain high levels of caffeine and can be dangerous if you drink them too often. Studies have shown they raise the heart rate by eight percent, and the effects can take hours to wear off.

ENERGY DRINKS CAN CAUSE PALPITATIONS—THE FEELING THAT YOUR HEART IS FLUTTERING OR POUNDING.

54

Extra help

Your heart beats because it receives small electrical signals. These stimulate the muscle and make it contract at regular intervals, to push the blood around. An electrocardiogram (ECG) can pick up these signals and record them on a chart, to check that the heart is beating as it should. A pacemaker is a small electrical box that can be fitted in the chest to help control an irregular heartbeat.

Feel the beat

You can feel (and count) your own heartbeat by finding your pulse. Blood pumping through blood vessels makes them expand and contract, which makes them pulse under your skin at the same rate as your heartbeat. Placing two fingers on a pulse point (where the vessel is near the surface) allows you to count how many beats you feel.

You have pulse points on your wrists and in your neck.

Listening in

A medic can check your heart rate with a stethoscope. A small disk is placed on your chest, with tubes leading to the doctor's ears. They will be able to hear a regular heartbeat, or clicks and swishes that suggest there is a problem. They can also count how many beats there are per minute.

FACT
46

The fastest heart rate possible is 220 beats per minute.

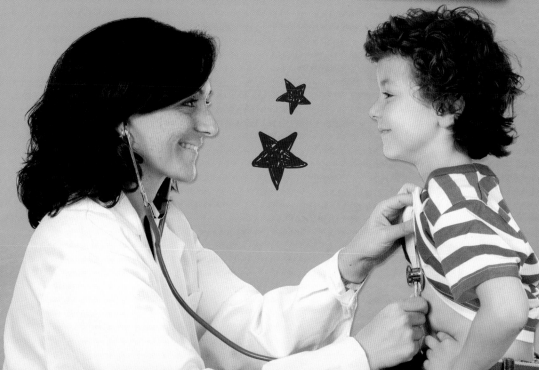

WHITE BLOOD CELLS EAT DISEASES!

White blood cells are constantly on the lookout for invaders. They attack bacteria and viruses to defend your body from diseases. Some of them swallow up these bad guys to stop you getting sick.

WHITE BLOOD CELLS LOOK LIKE A FUZZY BALL COMPARED TO SMOOTH RED BLOOD CELLS.

Under attack

White blood cells are part of your body's immune system, which defends your body from the germs that make you ill. White cells make up only 1 percent of your blood, and float around in a yellow substance called plasma. There are two types, lymphocytes and phagocytes, and each attacks unwanted organisms in a different way.

Gobble gobble!

Phagocytes are the hungry warriors in your blood. They can exit your blood vessels and roam around your body, looking for foreign organisms. When they find them, they pull them in and surround them, dissolving the intruder to prevent it doing you any harm. A single phagocyte can eat more than 100 bacteria before its short lifetime is over.

Pus is formed by dead phagocytes that fought an infection in the body.

Lock and key

Lymphocytes stay in the blood until foreign cells are detected. They attach onto the cell's surface with specially shaped proteins called antibodies. Each antibody fits onto a specific surface (called the antigen) like a key fitting the correct lock. Once they are locked together, the lymphocyte kills off bacteria and viruses, or destroys the body's own cells that have become infected or cancerous.

OVER HALF OF YOUR BLOOD IS MADE UP OF PALE YELLOW PLASMA.

Transport system

Plasma surrounds the other blood cells to transport them around the body. It carries many other things as well: hormones, minerals and salts, food, and waste products such as dead cells that need to be disposed of. It also carries platelets, which are the tiny cells that clot together to stop bleeding.

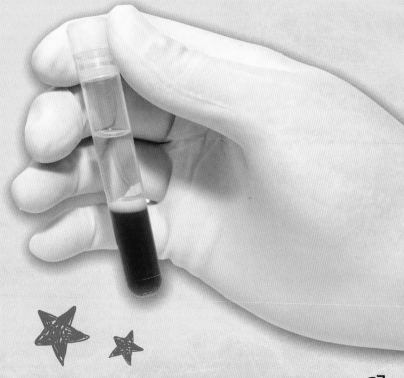

YOU BREATHE THROUGH ONE NOSTRIL AT A TIME

More than three quarters of the population naturally breathe through only one nostril. Usually, the nostrils take turns, swapping from working to resting every four hours or so.

One at a time

The inside of the nose has a soft lining that makes a protective goo, most commonly known as snot! This lining can swell and grow bigger to restrict the amount of air that goes up each nostril. Your nostrils take it in turns to do most of the breathing work, so each one gets a chance to rest. It usually happens without you thinking about it, just like the changes in your heart rate and digestion.

STUDIES SHOW THAT YOU USE MORE OXYGEN WHEN BREATHING THROUGH THE RIGHT NOSTRIL!

FACT 49

The visible divide between your nostrils is called your columella.

Newborn noses

Young babies breathe through their nose nearly all of the time. It helps when they are feeding. They lock their whole mouth in place as they drink their milk, and take in air through their nose. However, they breathe through their mouth if they are crying, and by the time they are a few months old they will switch to mouth breathing more often.

Babies snuffle and snort a lot to keep their nose clear!

THE SEPTUM DIVIDES YOUR NOSE INSIDE. IF THE BLOOD VESSELS BREAK, YOU GET A NOSE BLEED.

Cleaning up

The nostril lining is extremely useful. It warms and moistens the air before it enters your lungs. It also filters out unwanted particles such as dust, pollen, smoke, and germs, helping to keep your lungs clean and healthy. Small hairs called cilia at the very top of your nose help to make the air even cleaner.

FACT 50

The nose lining produces more moisture in cold weather, making your nose run.

Night night

Your nostrils take turns whether you are awake or asleep. If you are lying on your right side, your right nostril will close up, and vice versa. It is common to switch position during the night, so both nostrils will still do their night shift! Breathing through your mouth at night can lead to snoring, disturbed sleep, and a really dry mouth the next morning.

zzzzz

YOUR BODY CANNOT STORE OXYGEN

When you breathe in, you take air into your lungs. The lungs extract oxygen, which is vital for your body to function. You need a constant supply or you're in trouble!

Vital supplies

We need to breathe to stay alive. The process is called respiration, and it supplies vital oxygen to all parts of your body. You also need water and food, to provide vitamins, minerals, and fuel, but your body can store many of these things to use when it needs them. Oxygen cannot be stored, so you have to keep breathing constantly or you would die within minutes.

WHEN RESTING, A PERSON BREATHES IN AROUND 6 L (1.5 GALLONS) OF AIR EACH MINUTE.

Newborn noses

Young babies breathe through their nose nearly all of the time. It helps when they are feeding. They lock their whole mouth in place as they drink their milk, and take in air through their nose. However, they breathe through their mouth if they are crying, and by the time they are a few months old they will switch to mouth breathing more often.

Babies snuffle and snort a lot to keep their nose clear!

THE SEPTUM DIVIDES YOUR NOSE INSIDE. IF THE BLOOD VESSELS BREAK, YOU GET A NOSE BLEED.

Cleaning up

The nostril lining is extremely useful. It warms and moistens the air before it enters your lungs. It also filters out unwanted particles such as dust, pollen, smoke, and germs, helping to keep your lungs clean and healthy. Small hairs called cilia at the very top of your nose help to make the air even cleaner.

FACT 50

The nose lining produces more moisture in cold weather, making your nose run.

Night night

Your nostrils take turns whether you are awake or asleep. If you are lying on your right side, your right nostril will close up, and vice versa. It is common to switch position during the night, so both nostrils will still do their night shift! Breathing through your mouth at night can lead to snoring, disturbed sleep, and a really dry mouth the next morning.

zzzZZ

"BLACK EYES" CAN BE RED, PURPLE, OR YELLOW

Bruising around an eye can be alarming. Tiny blood vessels can break and bleed, causing the skin around the eye to turn bluish-red, before fading to brown and yellow.

Look out!

The eyes, and the area around them, are very delicate. The skin here is very thin, with blood vessels close to the surface. There are blood vessels in the whites of your eyes, and these can easily break, too. A smack in the eye or on the nose can cause damage, but so can smaller strains, even sneezing, coughing, vomiting, or blowing your nose!

I had a fight with a football, and the football won...

A BRUISE IS CAUSED BY BROKEN CAPILLARIES WHICH LEAK RED BLOOD CELLS.

Wearing the correct gear can protect you from injuries.

Ouch!

When you bang your leg or twist your ankle, it crushes the muscles and blood vessels inside. If the skin doesn't graze or break, the blood that escapes from the capillaries becomes trapped and forms the red mark that signals the beginning of a bruise.

Fade away

Bruises change shade as they heal. The initial red mark will turn purple and then blue or even black, as the blood is broken down and reabsorbed. As it gets older it will fade into green and yellow and finally a light brown, before it goes completely.

BRUISING HAPPENS MORE EASILY IF YOU DON'T HAVE ENOUGH VITAMIN C IN YOUR DIET.

Scabby skin!

What happens if the skin does get broken and blood leaks out? Your body needs to stop the blood from flowing, so it forms a hard, bumpy scab. This is the platelets in your blood (see page 57) sticking together. They bind with protein threads (called fibrin) and other blood cells to protect the wound from germs and allow new skin cells to grow underneath.

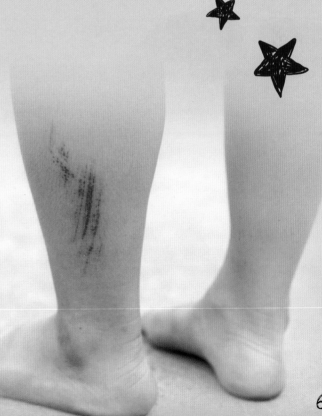

YOUR BODY CANNOT STORE OXYGEN

When you breathe in, you take air into your lungs. The lungs extract oxygen, which is vital for your body to function. You need a constant supply or you're in trouble!

Vital supplies

We need to breathe to stay alive. The process is called respiration, and it supplies vital oxygen to all parts of your body. You also need water and food, to provide vitamins, minerals, and fuel, but your body can store many of these things to use when it needs them. Oxygen cannot be stored, so you have to keep breathing constantly or you would die within minutes.

WHEN RESTING, A PERSON BREATHES IN AROUND 6 L (1.5 GALLONS) OF AIR EACH MINUTE.

In and out

Respiration starts with breathing in. The air travels to your lungs, where the oxygen is extracted and fed into the blood that has been pumped from the heart. The newly oxygenated blood passes back to the heart, to be sent on its way around the body. That's only half of the process, though. The blood from the heart contains carbon dioxide, which you need to get rid of by breathing out.

Water from your lungs escapes when you breathe out.

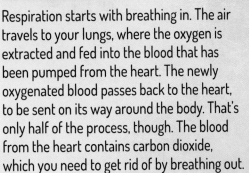

THERE ARE NO MUSCLES INSIDE THE LUNGS. THE DIAPHRAGM MAKES THEM EXPAND.

Branching out

The respiratory system begins with your mouth and nose, where you take in air. It passes down a tube in your throat and chest called the windpipe or trachea. This divides into two bronchi to get to both lungs. Inside each lung, the bronchi split into smaller tubes called bronchioles, like the branches and twigs on a tree.

Packing them in

The lungs aren't a big empty space inside; they are more like sponges than balloons. Each contains millions of tiny spaces, or sacs, called alveoli. These contain capillaries that absorb the oxygen into the blood. Around 300 million alveoli provide a huge surface area—nearly half a tennis court, if they were spread out—to fit in the maximum amount of capillaries.

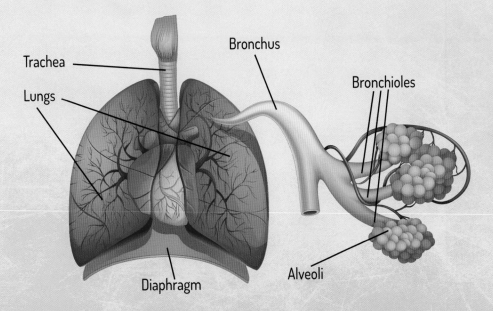

Trachea

Bronchus

Bronchioles

Lungs

Alveoli

Diaphragm

BREATHING ONLY FILLS YOUR LUNGS BY 8 PERCENT

Breathing out doesn't empty your lungs. Some air remains to keep them inflated. Even deep breathing uses only a small amount of the total volume inside.

Lung capacity

Each lung can hold up to 6 l (10 pints) of air, depending on the size of the person. However, we only breathe a small amount of this (about 8 percent, or 0.5 l/1 pint). If you exercise, you breathe more deeply, taking in and expelling a larger volume of air—up to around 50 percent. Increasing your lung capacity is good for your health, and will help with activities such as playing an instrument, singing, or diving.

IT IS POSSIBLE TO LIVE WITH ONLY ONE LUNG.

In and out

Your body needs oxygen, but that isn't the most common gas in the air. Air is made up of 79% nitrogen, 20% oxygen, 0.04% carbon dioxide, and tiny amounts of water and other gases. You only extract about 4% of the oxygen when you breathe, so you exhale 79% nitrogen, 16% oxygen, and 4% CO_2 and other gases.

Air in a fire has less oxygen, so breathing apparatus is needed.

MUSCLES BETWEEN YOUR RIBS MAKE THEM EXPAND AND CONTRACT AS YOU BREATHE.

Danger zone

Your body won't allow you to hold your breath for too long because it is dangerous. The brain detects the rising levels of carbon dioxide, which is toxic, and sends a message that causes pain in your chest. This makes you exhale to get rid of the waste gas.

Left versus right

Your lungs both do the same job, but they are not the same size. The left one is smaller than the right, to allow space for your heart. Each lung is divided into sections called lobes. The left lung has only two, compared to three in the right.

I'm breathing at a rate of 30 bubbles per minute.

Growing up

FACT 54
YOU CAN SEE AN EGG CELL WITHOUT A MICROSCOPE

The female egg cell is the largest cell in the human body. It is about the size of a grain of sand. To make a baby, it needs to be fertilized by a sperm cell, which is one of the smallest in the body.

New life

The reproductive system allows people to make babies. Sex cells called gametes are produced: sperm cells from a man and egg cells from a woman. Once these meet and join, a new life is on its way. It will develop inside the mother and takes around 280 days before a baby is born.

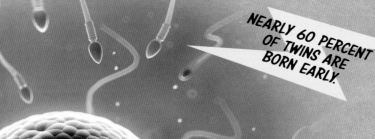

NEARLY 60 PERCENT OF TWINS ARE BORN EARLY.

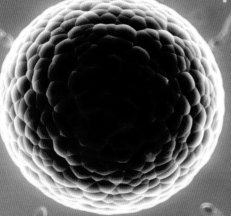

FACT 55

A human egg cell is about 100,000 times bigger than a sperm cell, by volume.

Most babies grow to over 2.5 kg (5.5 lb) before they are born.

A woman's role

When a girl reaches puberty (see page 76) she begins to release eggs from her ovaries. One egg is released each month, and if it is not fertilized it passes away when the girl has her period. A baby girl has eggs in her ovaries before she is even born. She may have a fixed number, although recent studies suggest that new eggs might be made through a woman's lifetime.

FACT
56

A human male makes around 1,500 sperm cells every second.

A man's role

Sperm cells are made inside a man's testes and released through the penis in a liquid called semen. Sperm really do look like tiny tadpoles. They have a head and a tail and have to swim to find the egg. Millions are released together and compete to get to the egg first.

Growing and growing

When a sperm and egg cell meet, they join to form a zygote. This divides over and over and turns into a fetus and the placenta, sitting in the woman's womb. After four weeks the cells separate into layers from which the baby's skin and internal organs will grow. By week six it has tripled in size, and by nine weeks it is about the size of a cherry.

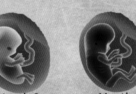

Month 1   Month 2   Month 3

Month 4   Month 5   Month 6

Month 7   Month 8   Month 9

FACT 57

WHITE BABIES ARE BORN WITH BLUE EYES

When a white baby is born, its eyes contain no melanin. The melanin deposits may gradually increase, changing the eyes to green or brown. Babies of Asian, Hispanic, or African descent have much more melanin, so usually have brown eyes at birth.

BLUE EYES ARE BECOMING LESS COMMON THROUGHOUT HISTORY.

Changes

Melanocytes are cells in the skin, hair, and eyes that produce melanin. The levels of melanin determine what shade our hair and eyes are, and the darkness of our skin. Dark-skinned people have more melanin than fair-skinned people. The amount of melanin in the iris of the eye can increase after birth when it is exposed to light, and change it from blue to various shades of green, hazel, or brown.

When I grow up, I want to have brown eyes!

Blurred vision

A newborn's eyes and brain don't see very well. The baby can make out light versus dark, and can see movement, and objects about 25 cm (10 in) away. As they develop, the eyes focus better and follow moving objects. By eight months, they can judge the position of an object, and see things across the room.

A young baby can see a parent's face at the right distance.

THE BIRTH RATE FOR TWINS HAS RISEN DRAMATICALLY OVER THE LAST FOUR DECADES.

Born together

It is becoming more common for a mother to give birth to twins: two babies born at the same time. If the zygote (fertilized egg) splits into two parts, the babies will be identical. Both grow together in the womb and have almost identical DNA, making them look virtually the same. However, because of the way melanin cells work, it is possible to have different eyes or hair!

Lots of babies

Sometimes, a woman may release two eggs and both are fertilized. They develop and are born together as twins, but as they didn't start from the same zygote, they don't look identical. It can even happen with three eggs (triplets) or more!

A BABY'S BRAIN SIZE TRIPLES IN ONE YEAR

A baby is born with a much smaller brain than an adult. It fits inside its tiny head, to make being born more practical. After birth, it is free to grow bigger and heavier. It reaches about three quarters of adult weight by the age of two.

A NEWBORN HAS MORE BRAIN CELLS THAN IT NEEDS, BUT MANY ARE LOST AS IT AGES.

Invisible growth

A baby's brain develops both in size and in the connections it makes. It learns and grows, taking in information from the world around it. At birth, the brain contains around 100 billion neurons. These fire and connect as the baby learns how to move in new ways, process what it sees, and feel and express its emotions.

Getting bigger

A baby's brain isn't the only thing to grow. Its body does, too. The many types of cell that make up different tissue (muscle, bone, nerves) divide and multiply. Bones get longer and proteins pack out new cells to bulk them up. From birth to age two, a child grows quickly. The body and legs grow faster than the head to catch up in the size stakes.

The first six months

At first, a baby becomes aware of itself and its surroundings. Its muscles get stronger and it waves its arms and legs and takes in sounds and smells. Then it learns to lift its own head and smile. By four months it will be putting things in its mouth to see how they feel or taste, and making babbling noises. Its first teeth will begin to appear.

Babies can sit up and eat soft food at six months.

A BABY'S HEAD IS ABOUT ONE QUARTER OF ITS OVERALL SIZE.

Happy birthday!

Most babies crawl before they can walk, but by about one year old they will try to totter on their own two feet. They also say their first words around their first birthday, copying common sounds such as "da-da" and "ma-ma" and taking turns to make conversational noises.

71

YOUR BODY MAKES A BILLION CELLS A MINUTE

Your body's cells don't last your whole lifetime. They are constantly growing, wearing out, and dying. New ones replace the old ones at the rate of millions per second.

Life cycle

Life takes its toll on your cells, and most types need to be replaced along the way. Cells have different life spans: red blood cells last around four months, and white blood cells for more than a year. Skin cells live around two to three weeks, but sperm cells live for only three days. Some types don't get renewed. For example, brain cells and nerve cells can die but are not replaced.

THE LONGEST CELLS ARE NEURONS, WHICH CAN STRETCH HALF YOUR BODY LENGTH.

1, 2, 3–this could take a while.

Brothers and sisters share around half of their genes.

Cell division

Cells divide in two different ways. When more cells are needed, for growing and repairing, mitosis takes place. The vital ingredients are copied within the cell, then it divides into two identical cells. Meiosis is needed for reproduction. The ingredients inside pair off and divide twice to make four gametes (male or female sex cells). This way, each of us is a unique combination of genetic instructions.

Super cells

Most of the body's cells have special tasks and cannot swap around. A skin cell cannot become another type of cell during mitosis. However, special cells called stem cells can develop into most or any type of cell. They are found in bone marrow and in an unborn baby as its own cells divide and grow. Stem cells may be used to treat brain diseases such as Parkinson's, and other medical conditions.

Getting old

Although the body produces new cells, we still show signs of aging. New cells perform less well as you get older, possibly because of outside factors such as sunlight, poor diet, and pollution. We also lose some cells, making our body less able to repair its joints, organs, and muscles.

YOUR ARM SPAN IS THE SAME AS YOUR HEIGHT

When you are fully grown, the distance between your outstretched hands should roughly equal your height. The arm span is often slightly less when you are growing, until you reach the age of ten or eleven.

Measuring up

We are clearly all different; some people have different proportions, with long arms or short bodies or little legs. Many people have the same proportions but vastly different heights. It's all down to our genes, passed on from our parents. Genes determine how tall we are, the shade of our eyes, skin, and hair, and even whether we have dimples, freckles, or crooked teeth.

YOU ARE ABOUT
SEVEN TIMES TALLER
THAN THE LENGTH OF
YOUR FOOT.

Blame your parents

Genes are located within your body's cells. They are sets of instructions on how you look, what illnesses you might have, and how you act. You inherit one set of genes, a genome, from each parent. Mixing genomes during reproduction guarantees diversity throughout a species.

Pairs of instructions

Cells contain more than 25,000 genes each. They are located on 23 pairs of chromosomes—half from each parent. Chromosomes are made of an acid called DNA, and look a bit like spaghetti. They combine to determine whether you are male or female, as well as all of your physical characteristics.

Genes determine whether you can roll your tongue like this!

Born this way?

There is much debate about the influence genes have on talents and personality. Scientists constantly study and discuss whether genes determine if you will be good at activities such as chess, music, sport, or learning a language. They have also put forward a theory that there is a "practice" gene that makes you more likely to try over and over until you improve.

DNA STANDS FOR DEOXYRIBONUCLEIC ACID, AND THERE ARE 2 M (6.5 FT) COILED INSIDE EACH CELL.

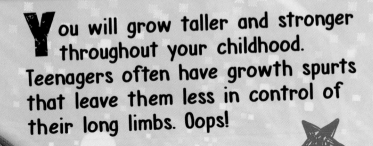

GROWING CAN MAKE YOU CLUMSY!

You will grow taller and stronger throughout your childhood. Teenagers often have growth spurts that leave them less in control of their long limbs. Oops!

What's happening?

The teenage years are a time of immense change. Puberty kicks in as the body prepares for adulthood. Teenagers do much of their growing at this stage, too. This growth doesn't happen in a smooth, even way. It often comes in leaps and bounds known as growth spurts, and makes motor skills harder. The brain takes time to adjust to the added height, bigger feet, and changed dimensions of the body.

FACT 62 Girls tend to stop growing by age **18**, while boys keep going until they're about **20**.

THE HANDS AND FEET ARE THE FIRST PARTS OF THE BODY TO GET BIGGER DURING PUBERTY.

Growing pains

Growing at accelerated speeds can have side effects. Not only might you be clumsier than usual, but it can hurt sometimes. Many 8- to 12-year olds feel cramping or throbbing in their leg muscles. A condition known as Osgood-Schlatter disease causes knee pain, usually because of overuse of the joints during sports while the body is growing and changing.

Changing times

Puberty starts when special hormones are released from the pituitary gland in your brain. Some of these are growth hormones; others make surprising things like body hair and pimples appear. It usually begins at around age 11 for girls, and from age 12 for boys, but it can happen any time between about eight and 14.

Special medical tape can support the knee during sports.

THE ACHILLES TENDON AT THE BACK OF THE LEG IS THE THICKEST IN THE BODY.

Going up!

A growth spurt can make your feet a few sizes bigger in as many months, or see your height shoot rapidly up. While normal growth differs from person to person, an average height increase of around 6 cm (2.5 in) per year is most likely between age 2 and age 10. That can zoom to over twice as much in a growth spurt.

My feet are farther away these days...

PUBERTY RESHAPES YOUR BRAIN

It's not only the teenage body that has growth spurts. The brain does, too. The volume of the outer layer (the cortex) increases in your early teens, and different areas mature and develop as you approach adulthood.

Brain changing

The brain has two major periods of development, once as a toddler and again as an adolescent. During these growth spurts the brain increases its processing power and makes countless new connections. Early areas of development in a toddler's brain include movement and sensing the outside world. The last parts to change, even after your teenage years, are the areas needed for planning ahead and controlling your emotions and impulses.

THE CORTEX GROWS THICKER DURING TEEN YEARS, AND THEN BECOMES THINNER AGAIN.

Danger zone

The areas that deal with emotions, memories, and how you behave are scattered around the brain, but are often referred to overall as the limbic system. A teenager's growing brain learns how to deal with anger, pleasure, and fitting in with friends. It can be a dangerous time when thrill-seeking takes over, before the adult functions of risk assessment and consequences are fully developed.

It is hard to juggle new emotions about the world you live in.

Crazy times

So, that's the hidden, mental side of things. What about your outward appearance? New hormones also trigger acne, the growth of extra body hair, and unusual body smells. Great! Both boys' and girls' bodies get fuller and wider, with broader shoulders for boys and curvier hips and breasts for girls.

See, hear!

One small but significant body part grows larger during puberty: the voicebox. It has a noticeable effect, by making the voice deeper. A girl's voice gets slightly deeper but it can be a big change for a boy, known as his voice "breaking." A boy's voice can change from high to low and back again as it breaks.

THE ENLARGED VOICEBOX SOMETIMES SHOWS AT THE FRONT OF THE THROAT, AS THE ADAM'S APPLE.

HUMANS ARE AT THEIR PEAK AT AGE 25

The human body grows and gets stronger for the first 25 years. Bones are at their densest, muscles are strongest, the brain is at its best, and even the eyes and ears perform better than in later years.

Top performance

For the first two decades, a person's body and brain are growing and developing in so many ways. Professional athletes in their twenties combine maximum body strength and power, endurance, quick reactions, good eyesight, and the maturity and commitment to train in a structured way. It isn't all about sports, however. The twenty-something brain is best at problem solving, lateral thinking, and committing facts to memory.

STUDIES SHOW THAT YOU HAVE THE MOST FRIENDS WHEN YOU ARE ABOUT 25 YEARS OLD.

Building bones

A child's bones make new cells so their bones grow longer and stronger. They increase in density until they reach their maximum bone mass, between the ages of 18 and 25. After that, bone cells can still be added, but more are lost. Building strong bones in your youth means you have better reserves of bone mass for when you are older. A healthy diet (with lots of calcium and vitamins) and weight-bearing exercise (running, dancing, skipping, and team sports) will make your bones stronger.

Go to school!

School-age children are in their prime learning years for many reasons. The brain forms new connections all the time, allowing us to learn other languages, remember facts, and process and recall information quickly. But tell your parents not to worry: vocabulary and emotional intelligence continue to improve with age.

Friends and family

Recent studies into phones and social networks have found that 25-year-olds have the most friends. They talk to the most people, and for the longest amount of time. This social circle decreases with age as other commitments, such as work and having a family, take up more time. Contacts are lost and we rely on a smaller group of really close friends.

People under the age of 25 spend the most time meeting and talking.

YOU HAVE AS MANY HAIRS AS A CHIMP!

A human being has around 5 million hairs on his or her body. They cover the skin, except on the lips, palms, and soles of the feet. A chimp has a similar number, but they are darker and thicker.

A warm coat

There is a simple reason why mammals have hair on their body: to keep them warm. However, humans have developed to live in many different environments at a wide range of temperatures. A thick coating of hair would stop us from sweating as efficiently, and make our body overheat, so thinner hair has worked out as the best solution. We wear clothes to help keep us warm instead.

WE LOSE UP TO 100 HAIRS A DAY FROM OUR HEAD.

FACT
66

Hair grows faster than fingernails.

Hair care

Some of your hairs protect you, rather than keeping you warm. Hairs in your nose prevent small particles such as dust, pollen, and smoke from entering your respiratory system and causing irritation. Your eyelashes do a similar job, keeping out dirt, and stopping evaporation that would dry out your eye surface. Eyebrows channel sweat and rain away from your eyes so you can see clearly. Eyelashes and eyebrows reduce the glare of bright light into your eyes, too.

Eyebrows play a big part in showing your emotions.

All rise!

The hairs on your arms and legs do try to keep you warm, even though they are poorly designed for the job. Tiny muscles in your skin contract and make the hairs stand on end, giving you those familiar goosebumps. With thicker hair, this would trap air to stop heat escaping.

Lovely locks

Each hair grows out of a tiny tube in the skin, called a follicle. Blood vessels at the base of the tube supply oxygen and food for the hairs to grow. The shape and size of the follicle makes your hair straight or curly, and fine or thick. A sebaceous gland at the root releases oil to keep your hair shiny and resistant to water. Too much oil will give you greasy hair, but too little makes it dry and brittle.

FACT 67

Round follicles give straight hair, while flat follicles make hair curly.

FEET AND HANDS HAVE THE MOST SWEAT GLANDS

Sweating is your body's way of cooling down. Droplets evaporate from the skin, taking heat with them. Your palms and soles have more sweat-producing glands than other areas of the body.

WOMEN HAVE MORE SWEAT GLANDS THAN MEN, BUT MEN'S ARE MORE ACTIVE.

FACT

69

Modified sweat glands in your ears produce earwax.

Sweat it out

Sweat is produced by glands located deep inside your skin. They carry liquid to the skin's surface along a tube or duct. There are around 370 sweat glands on your palms and soles on an area the size of your little fingernail, compared to around 175 on your forehead and only 60–80 on your legs and back. Sweating is triggered by exercise, hot air, or by fear and anxiety.

Cooling down

The human body is covered with 2-5 million sweat glands. Some are more active than others, which is why some people are sweatier than other people. Your body can produce two types of sweat. The first comes from eccrine glands, and the liquid released is mostly water, salt, and potassium. If you move from a cold climate to a hot one, your body will learn to double the amount of sweat it can produce.

Fit people start to sweat earlier, as their body knows instantly what to do.

FACT 70 Caffeine can increase the amount you sweat.

Stinky sweat

Apocrine glands release liquid through hair follicles, so are concentrated around the body's hairiest parts: the groin, underarms, and scalp. The liquid they produce contains fatty acids and proteins, which combine with bacteria on the skin to make the sweat smell. It evaporates more slowly, and can make a yellowish stain on your clothes. That is why we target our underarms with antiperspirant and deodorant.

DOGS HAVE FEW SWEAT GLANDS, SO THEY PANT TO COOL DOWN.

Sweaty palms

Eccrine glands work all the time to keep you cool, but apocrine glands only kick in at puberty. Yet again, it's down to hormones, which send signals around your body that it's time for a change. Sweat glands are stimulated by the nervous system, so you can be in a cold room, but anxious about meeting someone or giving a presentation, and your body will still release sweat.

Healthy bodies

FACT 71

YOUR SKIN IS LIKE A DUVET!

Your skin keeps you warm and safe, just like a snuggly bedcover. Not only that, but if you were to lay an adult's skin out flat, it would be about the size of a single bed!

Gift wrapped

Your skin is your largest organ. It covers the whole body, but if an adult's skin was laid out flat (ugh) it would have an area of about 2 m^2 or 21 square feet. It holds all your vital parts in, and keeps any nasty things out. It is waterproof, to stop your body becoming saturated, and it acts as a filter for the harmful rays of the Sun.

FACT 72

The skin is thinnest on your eyelids, and thickest on the soles of your feet.

AN ADULT'S SKIN WEIGHS ABOUT THE SAME AS TEN BASKETBALLS.

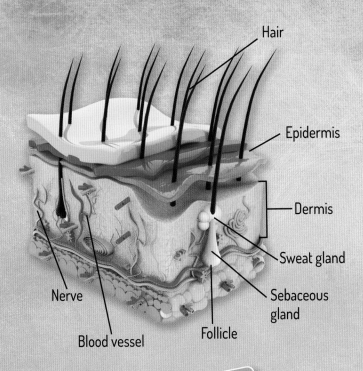

Hair

Epidermis

Dermis

Sweat gland

Sebaceous gland

Nerve

Blood vessel

Follicle

Tough on the outside...

The outer layer of the skin is called the epidermis. It is tough but flexible, so you can bend and stretch. The epidermis completely replaces itself every month, shedding old cells and replacing them with new ones. Dead skin flakes fall from its surface all the time, and are eaten by tiny creatures called dust mites. Yum!

...tender on the inside

The layer beneath the surface is known as the dermis. It is where blood vessels, nerves, sweat glands, hair follicles, and sebaceous glands are found. It is much thicker than the outer layer and acts as a cushion, regulates your body temperature, and generates your sense of touch.

FACT 73

We shed around 20 kg (44 lb) of dead skin in a lifetime.

Save your skin

The epidermis contains melanin (see page 68) which filters out dangerous ultraviolet (UV) rays from the Sun. Darker skin is more effective at this task, which is why people with pale skin get sunburn more easily. Too much UV radiation can damage the DNA of your cells, leading to skin cancer.

Stay well protected with sunblock, hats, and light clothes.

YOUR FEET ARE COVERED IN BACTERIA

Billions of bacteria cells make their home on just one foot! There are around 1,000 kinds of bacteria living all around your body. Some of them are bad for you, but others have an important job to do.

Tiny terrors

Bacteria are tiny living cells, or microorganisms. Those from outside the body can cause sore throats, food poisoning, and other serious diseases such as pneumonia and meningitis. But "good" bacteria live inside your mouth, your gut, and on your skin. Your feet are a prime target for trapped bacteria, as they are usually inside socks, shoes, or tucked up in your bed.

BACTERIA CAN BE FOUND IN SOIL, AIR, FRESH WATER, THE OCEANS, THE EARTH'S CRUST, AND EVEN RADIOACTIVE WASTE.

Foot foes

Some of the bacteria that live on your feet eat the oils and dead skin cells. They love the moist, dark conditions inside sweaty shoes and multiply fast. These bacteria can make your feet stinky. Others cause an infection that gives a sore, red rash between your toes. It looks similar to athlete's foot but needs different treatment, as athlete's foot is caused by a fungus, not bacteria. Equally unpleasant!

Go barefoot when possible, and keep your feet clean and dry.

AN ESTIMATED 600 SPECIES OF BACTERIA LIVE INSIDE YOUR MOUTH.

The good guys

The digestive system needs bacteria to break down food and absorb the nutrients. Bacteria also help to produce some of the vitamins you need (such as B and K) and kill off harmful bacteria to stop you getting sick. Certain species help to dispose of drugs and hormones that aren't needed any longer.

The bad guys

Scientists suggest there are more than 500 million bacteria in every teaspoon of spit. These can cause tooth decay and gum disease if you allow them to linger and become plaque; that's why it is important to brush regularly. Other harmful bacteria can be breathed in and swallowed, but they are usually attacked by enzymes in saliva or the stomach.

VIRUSES PLAY HIDE AND SEEK IN YOUR BODY

Unlike bacteria, viruses are not living cells, but they are sneaky. Once they have invaded your body, they can mutate (change) and hide from the body's defensive system.

Hitching a ride

Viruses are much smaller than bacteria (up to 100 times smaller) but they cannot thrive on their own. They have to get inside a living cell to be able to grow. The virus reproduces and spreads to other cells, but our bodies learn how to defend against it. In order to survive, the virus has to change so that it can trick other cells into letting it through their "screening" process.

SCIENTISTS KNOW OF ABOUT 4,000 VIRUSES BUT BELIEVE THERE MAY BE AS MANY AS 400,000 TYPES ON EARTH.

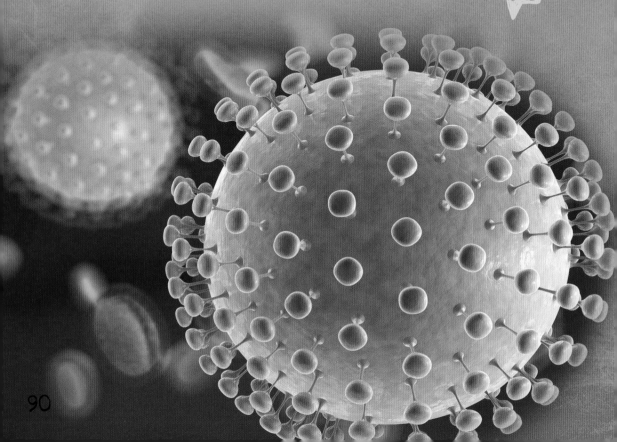

On the move

Diseases—both viral and bacterial—can spread from person to person very easily. They are passed on by coughing and sneezing germs for someone else to breathe in. You can also transfer them from surfaces; for example, if you touch a door handle with a virus on it, and then touch your nose or mouth. The flu virus can survive for up to 48 hours on items such as door handles and keyboards. Ugh!

A remote control could have more than 1,000 bacteria on one button.

Animal illness

Some viruses are fussy about what or whom they infect: for example, a plant virus will only infect another plant. Unfortunately, many viruses that start in animals can adapt to humans. Outbreaks of serious diseases such as Ebola and HIV began in animals, probably bats and chimpanzees. Influenza (the flu) can move across from pigs and birds. Rabies is passed on through a bite from an infected animal. These animal-to-human viruses are called zoonotic.

Hiding everywhere

Like bacteria, viruses can be found in the soil, air, water, ice: anywhere they can hope to find a living host.

THE COMMON COLD CAN BE CAUSED BY MORE THAN 200 DIFFERENT VIRUSES.

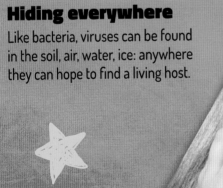

YOUR BODY IS A WAR ZONE!

Your body is always fighting to protect itself. You have a whole system just to keep you safe from invaders, and it is called the immune system.

Fighting fit

Your immune system starts on the surface: your skin. This defends you against many nasties, unless it becomes damaged by a cut or a graze. Deep inside, white blood cells (see page 56) destroy any diseases that sneak past your defensive barriers. The immune system has many other weapons to wage war on all the tiny single-cell organisms that can cause you harm, such as bacteria, viruses, and fungi (collectively called microbes).

I see a virus. Attack! Attack!

MICROBES ARE SO TINY THAT MILLIONS COULD FIT ONTO THE MIDDLE OF THIS O.

Ready for battle

When the immune system detects foreign invaders, it produces antibodies to kill off infected cells and stop the disease from spreading. These antibodies stay in your body in case the same germs invade again. Then your body is ready to fight them off, even faster than before.

Polio, tetanus, measles, and mumps can be prevented with vaccinations.

Future protection

Vaccinations help your body to fight off dangerous diseases. A small amount of a weakened disease is injected into the body. The immune system responds with antibodies to kill it off, and these antibodies remain in case a full-blown version of the disease tries to take hold at a later date.

Slime wars

Some of the body's best warriors are wet or slimy! Special tissue called mucus membrane lines your eyes, nose, mouth, and digestive system. It keeps them moist by producing a thick protective fluid that stops microbes from entering and harming the body. The stomach lining works extra hard to stop us digesting harmful substances.

SALIVA AND TEARS CONTAIN AN ENZYME THAT DESTROYS MICROBES.

YOU CAN BE ALLERGIC TO YOUR PHONE

Imagine never being able to text or talk on your phone again! Many phones contain the metals nickel, chromium, and cobalt in the casing, and these can cause skin allergies such as swelling, blisters, or a rash. Disaster!

ONE OF THE MOST COMMON ALLERGIES IS HAYFEVER, A REACTION TO PLANT POLLEN.

A is for allergy

Many of us react to certain foods, plants, animals, perfumes, metals, or chemicals with itchy red patches or bumpy, inflamed skin. This is an allergic reaction, and it can also cause sneezing, itchy eyes, a runny nose, sickness, or difficulty breathing. The symptoms can be irritating, but in some cases they are life-threatening.

NOOOOOOOOOOOO!

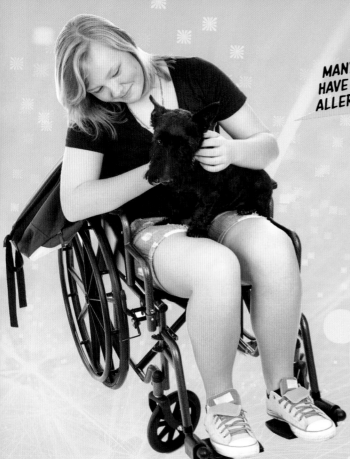

Mistaken identity

The body produces antibodies to fight off invaders, but sometimes they get it wrong. They can overreact to harmless substances, and attack them as if they were germs. The antibodies make some cells release histamine into the blood. This substance brings on the symptoms of a reaction, and it will happen again whenever the trigger (known as an allergen) is encountered.

Danger zone

Allergic reactions can be annoying, but some can be much more serious. They can close up the airways and make it hard to breathe. Occasionally, an allergy can cause anaphylactic shock. The person's lips, tongue, and throat swell up until they cannot breathe or swallow, and they feel weak or faint.

Take a breath

Asthma is a common disease that affects breathing. Sufferers feel wheezy and tight-chested, especially after exercise or in cold air. If you are asthmatic, an attack can often be triggered by an allergic reaction. An inhaler squirts medicine directly into the airways to help make breathing easier.

An asthma sufferer will often find they are allergic to dust, fur, and pollen.

TEETH CAN SHOW HOW OLD YOU ARE

Your adult teeth arrive by your early teens and should stay with you your whole life. Even after death, teeth can give clues about ancient remains. They can show age, diet, disease, and ethnic background.

Growing and changing

Most children get wobbly teeth when they are about five years old. Gradually, the baby teeth fall out and are replaced by a permanent set of adult teeth. These are usually yellower and much bigger, with a bumpy biting edge. This is worn away as you get older. Changes such as these, and tooth decay, give historians clues when they find ancient remains.

IN 2015, A HUMAN TOOTH OVER HALF A MILLION YEARS OLD WAS FOUND IN FRANCE.

Look! No tooth!

FACT
79

Children have a set of 20 teeth, but adults can have up to 32.

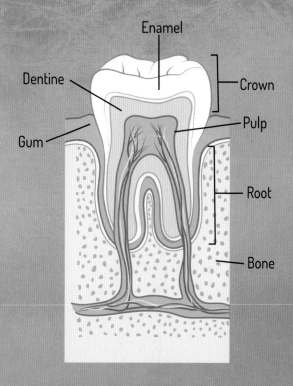

Enamel

Dentine

Gum

Crown

Pulp

Root

Bone

Open wide!

The visible part of a tooth is called the crown. It is held in place in the gum by its root. The hard outer layer of the crown is made of enamel. Underneath is a thick layer of dentine, surrounding the inner pulp which contains nerves and blood vessels. The pulp goes all the way down through the root.

Mapping it out

Teeth are made of tough stuff but they do get ground down with use. Studies of ancient teeth look at wear and tear and cavities to see how old a person was when they died. They can also give lifestyle clues, such as whether groups of people smoked pipes, used their teeth as tools, and what their geographical or ethnic background was.

FACT 80

Tooth enamel is the hardest substance in the body, even stronger than bones.

You are what you eat

Human habits alter through history, and experts can find patterns of change in ancient teeth. They show what kind of foods people ate the most: tough, woody foods they found as hunter-gatherers, or softer, sugary and starchy fruits and vegetables grown in a farming society.

Sugar-coated fruit will show up on your dental history!

TOOTH DECAY CAN KILL YOU!

It might sound crazy, but an untreated tooth infection really can kill, in extreme cases. The bacteria that eat away at your teeth can spread around your body with deadly results.

You do NOT want this

Bacteria in the mouth love to feed on sugary substances. This can cause holes in the teeth, gum disease, or abscesses: a nasty collection of pus inside a tooth, in the gum, or in the bones of your jaw. Any of those can be extremely painful. In rare cases, the bacteria find their way into the blood stream and can travel around the body, leading to organ failure.

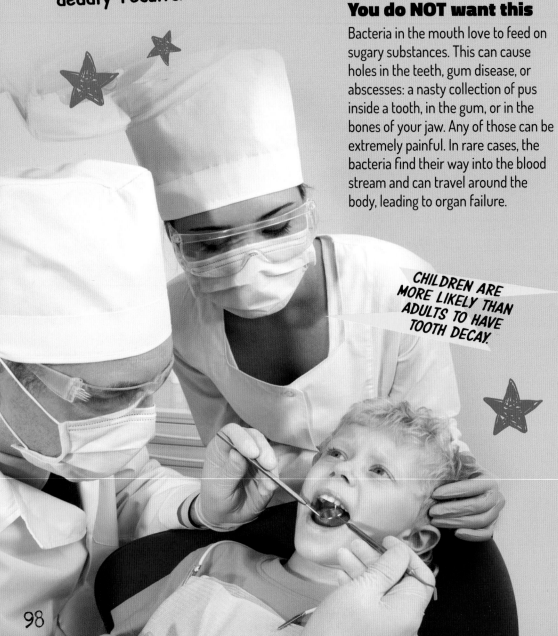

CHILDREN ARE MORE LIKELY THAN ADULTS TO HAVE TOOTH DECAY.

Brush away

Sugary or starchy foods build up inside the mouth, forming a coating called plaque. It is sticky but see-through and can feel like a furry layer. When bacteria feed on plaque, they release acids that eat into tooth enamel. It is vital that you brush your teeth twice a day, taking care to brush between any gaps and onto your gums.

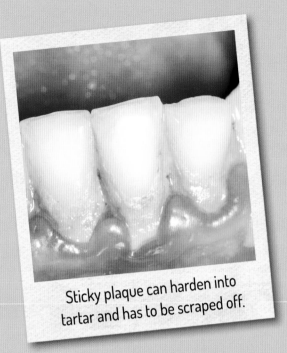

Sticky plaque can harden into tartar and has to be scraped off.

THE FIRST TOOTHBRUSHES HAD BRISTLES MADE FROM PIG HAIRS!

Bite, tear, crush, chew

Humans have different types of teeth for different purposes. The top and bottom two, at the front, are incisors, for biting into food. Next to those are the pointed canines, for tearing and gripping. You have flat-topped teeth at the sides of the mouth. First are the premolars, for crushing. Behind are the largest teeth, the molars, for grinding and chewing.

Gone forever

Teeth are unlike most of our terrific body parts—they can't repair themselves. The enamel coating is not living tissue, so it cannot mend and regrow. That's why it is so important to take good care of adult teeth. The molars are especially prone to decay as their design allows food to stick easily to the top surface.

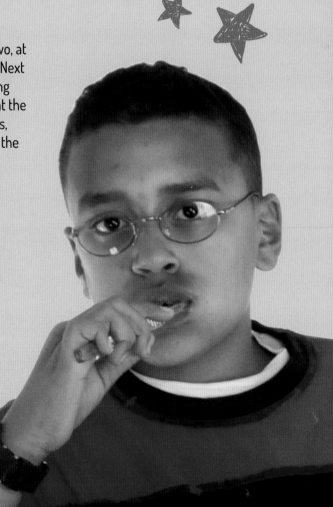

GIANT TAPEWORMS CAN LIVE IN YOUR GUT

Tapeworms are the longest human parasite, and may grow up to 12 m (40 feet) long. That's longer than seven adult humans lying end to end! They can be passed to humans from infected animals.

Living inside

A parasite is a creature that lives on or inside another creature. Tapeworms attach themselves to the inner wall of a person's intestines and feed off the food there. They are more common in developing countries, as they are spread by unhygenic living conditions. The worms get into their human host in food or water. Fortunately, tapeworms are easily treated with tablets.

TAPEWORMS ARE MADE OF SEGMENTS, AND GROW NEW SEGMENTS TO GET LONGER.

Blood-suckers

Lice also prey on people, biting their skin and sucking their blood. They are wingless insects, and different species live on different parts of the body. Head lice are common, especially in school children, where they spread easily from head to head. Fleas (shown here) are also insects that can jump onto human hosts from animals, and give a nasty bite.

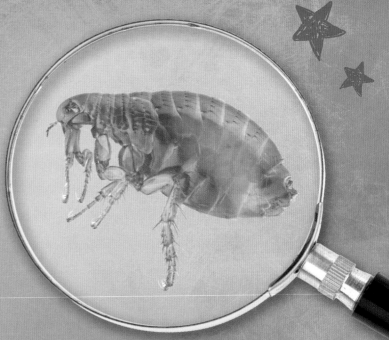

You might have mites

Not all parasites are big—some are tiny. Microscopic eight-legged creatures called mites use humans as hosts. Some of them come from animals and their bites can cause an itchy rash. Others feed on dead skin cells and old oils in hair follicles. They are called demodex mites and live in eyelashes and eyebrows without us even knowing they're there.

A FEMALE FLEA CAN DRINK 15 TIMES ITS OWN BODYWEIGHT IN BLOOD EVERY DAY.

Deadly diseases

Mosquitoes are members of the fly family that breed in non-flowing water such as ponds and gutters. They have tubelike mouthparts to pierce your skin and suck up blood. Many people are allergic to mosquito bites, and get a round, puffy bump that becomes hot and red. Some mosquitoes carry deadly diseases such as malaria, which has killed millions of people.

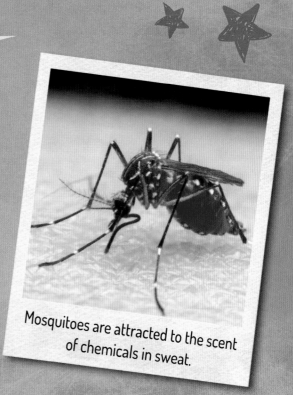

Mosquitoes are attracted to the scent of chemicals in sweat.

FACT 83 YOUR LIVER CAN REGROW ITSELF

The liver is an amazing organ. It performs more than 500 jobs inside the body. If it is damaged, or part of it has to be surgically removed, it can increase its cell growth to return to its original size.

AS LITTLE AS ONE QUARTER OF A LIVER CAN REGROW INTO A WHOLE LIVER.

Fighting back

The liver works extremely hard to keep your body functioning. If cells are destroyed (by disease, aging, or toxins such as alcohol and drugs) the liver can regrow new cells really quickly. But the liver is even more adaptable than other body parts. If a section is taken away, the remaining liver cells multiply to fill the space again.

POWER LIVER!

Excessive protein in your diet can put pressure on your liver.

Under attack

Although the liver can regrow cells, it is vulnerable to some attacks. Too much alcohol can kill off the cells and build up scar tissue in their place, causing cirrhosis. Viruses such as hepatitis may invade the liver, leading to vomiting, exhaustion, and a peculiar yellow tone to the skin and whites of the eyes.

Proteins and poisons

Your blood can contain toxins from various sources. Some are external, such as alcohol, drugs, and medicines that you no longer need. Others are produced internally when proteins in food break down. The liver filters out the bad stuff and passes it into the blood as urea. The kidneys then turn urea into urine so it can be removed from your body.

EXTERNAL TOXINS INCLUDE INSECT STINGS AND PESTICIDES BREATHED FROM THE AIR.

A sticky business

A lesser-known function of the liver is making the proteins that are needed for the blood to clot. This is vital so you don't bleed nonstop when you cut yourself, and so blood doesn't leak out inside your body after surgery or with internal injuries.

LIMES CAN SAVE YOUR LIFE!

A lack of vitamin C can cause a dreadful disease called scurvy. Way back in the 1700s, a ship's doctor discovered that citrus fruits, especially limes, could prevent the disease and keep the sailors alive on long voyages.

Eat healthy

Our bodies produce many of the chemicals we need to function properly, but we need to get vitamins from the foods we eat. Vitamin C comes from citrus fruits and berries, among other things. Low levels of this vitamin causes scurvy which leads to weakness, gum disease, and death from bleeding or infection, but thankfully it is rare these days.

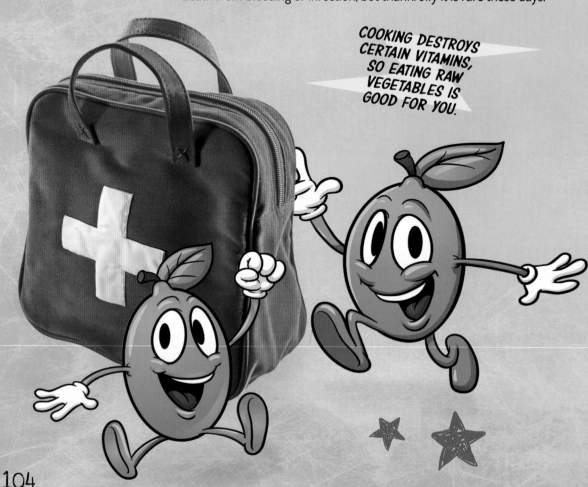

COOKING DESTROYS CERTAIN VITAMINS, SO EATING RAW VEGETABLES IS GOOD FOR YOU.

Eat a wide variety of foods to get all the vitamins you need.

Food stores

Some vitamins (A, D, E, and K) are fat-soluble and can be stored in your liver for when you need them. They are found mostly in dairy foods and oily fish. The B-vitamins, plus folic acid and vitamin C, are water-soluble so are passed out in your urine and you need to top them up regularly.

MINERALS ARE OFTEN ADDED TO CEREALS TO MAKE THEM A HEALTHY BREAKFAST CHOICE.

Sunshine vitamin

Vitamin D is different from most vitamins. It is found in fewer foods, but your body can make its own supplies from sunlight. It helps keep your bones strong and your muscles, lungs, and brain working at their best. Try to spend twenty minutes outdoors each day to top up your supplies.

Mineral marvels

We also need small amounts of minerals in our diet, particularly calcium (for our teeth and bones) and iron. Too little iron means our red blood cells are reduced in number so we receive less oxygen than we need. An iron deficiency makes you pale and tired, grumpy, out of breath, and can cause hair loss, headaches, and heart palpitations.

Mmmm, minerals...

FACT 85

COLD WEATHER CAN MAKE YOUR FINGERS FALL OFF

Extreme cold can freeze and damage skin cells. If the deeper tissue freezes, the area turns black as the cells die. This is called frostbite. Left untreated, victims may lose fingertips or toes.

FROSTBITE IS MORE LIKELY TO OCCUR AT HIGH ALTITUDES OR IN COLD WINDS.

Dangerous conditions

In extremely cold conditions, your body moves blood away from your extremities (fingers, toes, face, and ears) to your vital organs to keep them working. This leaves the extremities in a dangerous situation. Ice crystals form in the tissue, and the nerves and blood vessels are damaged. It starts with a tingling feeling but then turns numb. The skin turns black and the ends of fingers and toes may fall off.

The blood flow to the brain is reduced in extreme heat, making you feel faint.

Staying the same

The human body is meant to stay at a core temperature of 37°C (98.6°F), although your hands and feet can be colder than this. Temperature receptors in our skin pass messages to the brain about how hot or cold it is outside. An area of the brain called the hypothalamus processes the messages, and keeps our core temperature stable—for example, by making us sweat or shiver.

HEATSTROKE CAN OCCUR AT 40°C (104°F), WHEN YOUR BODY CANNOT REGULATE ITS OWN TEMPERATURE.

Way too hot

If the body becomes too hot, several things can happen. Sweating too much can lead to dehydration, which makes you weak and confused, and likely to faint or vomit. Heatstroke is very dangerous indeed. The victim can become unconscious, and the internal temperature can rise to a level that causes brain damage or even death.

Feeling feverish

Sometimes the hypothalamus receives messages that the body is infected, and it raises the core temperature to fight off diseases. This gives us a fever, making us sweat although we shiver and feel cold.

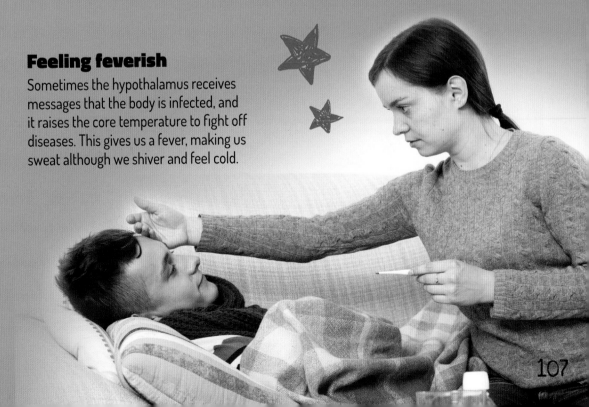

Eat up!

FACT 86 YOU EAT SIX ELEPHANTS IN A LIFETIME!

Well, clearly you don't eat actual elephants. But the total amount of food you eat weighs about the same as six elephants. You flush away waste products weighing between one and two elephants' weight.

Losing weight

So, what happens to the rest of the food? It gets digested and turned into energy (for moving and functioning), heat (to keep your body at the correct core temperature), and is lost as liquid. It is easy for an adult to sweat 1 l (0.25 gallons) of liquid per day, even in a moderate climate and without exercising. Add that to the liquid you lose when you breathe out and urinate, and it rises to around 2.5 l (0.66 gallons) per day.

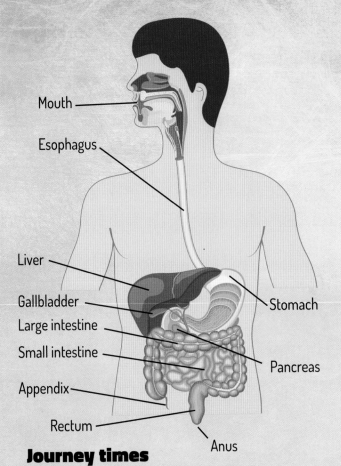

Mouth

Esophagus

Liver

Gallbladder

Large intestine

Small intestine

Appendix

Rectum

Stomach

Pancreas

Anus

Start to finish

Your mouth is the start of your digestive system. Chewed food passes into the throat and down a long tube to your stomach, then onto your intestines and out the other end. Other organs play their part: the pancreas makes juices that help the small intestine do its job, and the rectum stores waste until stretch receptors send signals to the brain that it is time to find a bathroom!

Journey times

After chewing for a few seconds, with a few seconds more in the journey downward, food then slows down. It stays in your stomach for two to four hours, depending on the kind of food it is. It spends another five or six hours in the small intestine, and up to a day in the large intestine. So your breakfast won't reappear until the morning after you ate it.

Food as fuel

Foods can be split into three general types: proteins, fats, and carbohydrates. They take different lengths of time to digest, so serve our body in different ways. Carbohydrates can be broken down and absorbed really quickly, giving you instant energy. Proteins are more complex so take longer, but keep you going as you work hard. Fats digest more slowly still and the body stores them in case it needs energy at a future point.

Athletes eat high-protein foods as they are a long-lasting source of fuel.

109

FACT 87 YOU HAVE FOUR KINDS OF TEETH

The process of digestion starts at your mouth. You have different types of teeth for cutting, tearing, grasping, crushing, and grinding food.

ONE THIRD OF A TOOTH IS HIDDEN FROM SIGHT, INSIDE THE GUMS.

Terrific teeth

The four types of teeth have different designs to suit their job. Incisors are chisel-shaped with a thin edge, for cutting. Canines are sharp and pointed for tearing. Premolars are diamond-shaped with two points on top, and molars are rectangular with a point at each corner. Pure carnivores such as lions have extremely well developed canines to handle all that raw meat. They can grow as long as your middle finger.

FACT 88

Eating parsley, apples, spinach, or mushrooms can fight bacteria that cause bad breath.

110

Mash up

Chewing is the first part of the digestive process. Your teeth mash food into smaller and smaller pieces to make them easier to swallow and digest. Saliva makes the food moist so it can be turned into a mushy ball (called a bolus) that moves easily through the digestive system.

Tongue twister

As you chew, your tongue pushes food around the mouth. It has a rough surface to help it to grip the bolus and eventually move it to the back to be swallowed. Swallowing happens without your thinking about it—it is one of the body's reflex actions.

Chewing slowly and steadily helps your digestion. Enjoy every mouthful!

EVERYONE HAS AN INDIVIDUAL TONGUE PRINT, MUCH LIKE A FINGERPRINT.

Cough and splutter

A flap of tissue, called the epiglottis, sits at the entrance to the throat and helps to stop you from choking on food. Your mouth opens into two tubes at the back, one for eating and one for breathing. The epiglottis stays open as you breathe, but closes as you swallow to direct food down the correct tube.

FACT
89
Swallowing uses around 50 pairs of muscles in your mouth and throat.

YOU MAKE FOUR BATHTUBS OF SPIT EACH YEAR

Spit, or saliva, is an extremely important substance. It helps you taste food, swallow food, and digest food. It is recycled as you swallow and reabsorb it, but adults can produce as much as 4 cups every day!

It starts with spit

Your digestive glands start working as soon as you smell or see food. Salivary glands in your mouth are activated by the very suggestion of your first bite. The saliva they produce is mostly water, with small amounts of mucus, white blood cells, and enzymes. These enzymes begin to break down the food as you chew. They work especially well on starchy carbohydrates, such as rice, pasta, and bread.

I'm well on my way to filling my first bathtub!

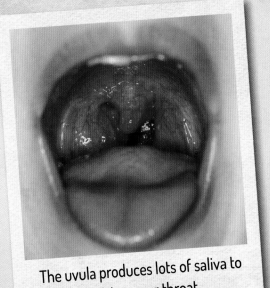

The uvula produces lots of saliva to moisten your throat.

What IS that?

If you look inside your own mouth in a mirror, you should be able to see a strange piece dangling at the back, like a small punchbag. That's your uvula. Scientists have pondered for years about its purpose, but they do know for sure that it closes your nasal cavity when you eat, to stop food going up your nose. It is also used in speech, to produce certain individual sounds.

WE PRODUCE LESS SALIVA WHILE WE ARE ASLEEP.

Super saliva

Saliva acts like your own personal mouthwash. It flushes out particles that could become stuck on your tongue and teeth. It also contains antibacterial substances that protect your teeth and gums. Sometimes, the tongue becomes coated with bacteria and dead cells, and turns white. If this happens, you should drink more water and concentrate on your dental hygiene.

Move along please

When your mouth has done its work, and you swallow food, it begins its journey to the stomach. It doesn't rely on gravity to work its way down. Instead, smooth muscles contract in waves, pushing the small ball of food along in the right direction. It even happens if you're lying down, the wrong way up, or an astronaut in a weightless environment.

FACT 91 STOMACH ACID CAN DISSOLVE METAL

The stomach is a bean-shaped sack that stores and breaks down food. It contains hydrochloric acid, which not only destroys bacteria and helps digestion, but is strong enough to dissolve bone, wood, and metal!

No need for food! I'll just eat the knife and fork.

Chemistry inside

The stomach is the first stopping point for your food. Digestion takes place here in two ways: chemically and physically. The stomach walls produces gastric juices: acid and enzymes that work on the food, helping to reduce it to a usable mush. The walls also contain epithelial cells, which make a protective lining that stops the stomach from dissolving itself.

FACT 92 A small person's stomach can be the same size as a large person's stomach.

THE STOMACH MAKES A NEW LINING ABOUT EVERY TWO WEEKS.

Heartburn

Many people suffer from heartburn (a burning feeling in the throat) and indigestion (a similar sensation in the tummy area). These are caused by stomach acid escaping into areas where it isn't wanted. Sometimes it is a result of eating too much or too fast and overloading the system. Occasionally it is because the stomach lining has been damaged.

Stomach acid can make you feel as if there's a fire inside you!

Mix it up

Physical digestion takes place in your stomach. Smooth muscles churn the food around, much like a washing machine, to help break it into smaller and smaller pieces, until it becomes a soupy liquid called chyme. Your stomach rumbles when you are hungry because there is no food to muffle the sound of these muscular motions.

Getting bigger

The stomach is extremely stretchy, to make room for large meals and lots of drinks. Before you eat, its volume is a measly 50 ml (1.7 fl oz) but it expands to around 1.5 l (50 fl oz) and then sends messages that you've eaten enough.

FACT
93

If pushed, the stomach can stretch up to 80 times its resting size!

THE SMALL INTESTINE IS ACTUALLY HUGE!

The small intestine is longer than the long intestine, but is named for its width, as it is much narrower. Stretched full length, an adult's small intestine would be more than three times taller than its owner!

Some statistics

The average length of an adult's small intestine is 6 m (20 ft) but the tube is only 2.5–3 cm (1 in) wide. In comparison, the large intestine is about 6–7 cm (2.5 in) wide but only 1.5 m (5 ft) long. The small intestine is curled around and around to fit inside the body, and the large intestine coils around it.

I've coiled up this long tube so I can carry it easily. Now where did I get that idea?

THE SMALL INTESTINE HAS A LARGE SURFACE AREA BUT IS CURLED UP INTO A SMALL SPACE.

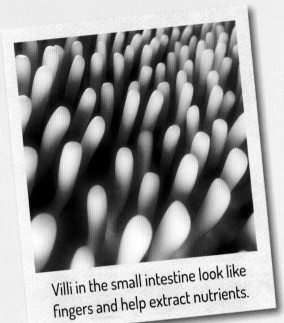
Villi in the small intestine look like fingers and help extract nutrients.

Getting the goodness

The small intestine's job is to extract nutrients from the chyme arriving from the stomach. These nutrients pass through the intestine walls and into the bloodstream. To make this process more efficient, the inside wall is lined with tiny villi. They increase the surface of the intestine, making its total area around half the size of a badminton court.

Waste disposal

Any undigested food carries on into your large intestine. Excess water is taken out and returned to your body. The products that are no use to you become solid waste. If they stay in the large intestine for too long, too much water is extracted and the waste becomes very hard. It is tricky to poop it out: a condition known as constipation.

A trip to the bathroom

The final parts of the digestive system are the rectum and the anus. Solid waste is stored in the rectum until it becomes full enough to send a message to the brain that you're ready to go to the toilet. The anus has muscles that control your pooping; they relax to open up and let you empty your system.

DUNG BEETLES FEED ON THE BITS OF NUTRITION LEFT IN ANIMAL WASTE.

FACT 95
THE LIVER IS AS BIG AS A PINEAPPLE

Your skin is your biggest organ, but the liver is the largest one inside your body. An adult's liver can be the size of a pineapple, and some of its functions will leave you needing the bathroom!

THE LIVER HAS TWO LOBES, AND THE RIGHT ONE IS MUCH LARGER THAN THE LEFT.

I'm desperate... I blame my liver!

Multitasking

The liver is a reddish-brown triangle and feels rubbery. You can't really touch it, as it sits behind the ribs on the right hand side, under the diaphragm and above the small intestine. It helps with blood clotting and removing toxins from the body (see page 103), but it also has various roles in digestion, from stockpiling nutrients to peeing and pooping!

Store cupboard

Blood that enters the liver contains high levels of glucose, broken down from the carbohydrates that we eat. The liver absorbs this glucose and stores it, ready to release in between meals when we need extra energy. It also stores many vitamins, minerals, and other nutrients carried in the blood.

Detox

The liver plays an extremely important role in removing toxins from the body. Some of these may be external, such as alcohol, drugs, or medicine that our body no longer needs. Others are produced internally when proteins are broken down. The waste is turned into urea in the liver and sent to the kidneys before passing out as urine.

The body uses its stores of glucose when it needs an energy boost.

MOST OF THE BODY'S WARMTH IS GENERATED BY THE LIVER.

Fatty foods

Bile is produced in the liver, and is vital for the digestive process. It breaks down fats into small pieces with more surface area, making them easier for the body to digest. Bile is a thick, greenish yellow liquid, which is stored just below in the gall bladder and released back into the liver as needed. Bacteria acts on bile to turn it brown before it mixes with solid waste and is disposed of.

FACT 96 YOU FART MORE THAN TEN TIMES A DAY!

It is perfectly normal to pass wind, although some people are more discreet about it than others. Whether you admit to it or not, you probably expel gas between ten and 14 times a day.

A windy day

Air is easily trapped inside the digestive system, and it makes us gassy. Some of it is swallowed when we eat and drink, some seeps from the blood into the intestines, but much of it is produced in our gut by chemical reactions. The good bacteria that break down food produce gas as a by-product, and it has to escape somehow or you will feel uncomfortable and bloated.

FACT 97 Only around one percent of the gas is smelly; the rest is stink-free.

CHEWING GUM CAN MAKE YOU MORE GASSY THAN NORMAL!

Super stink

Not all windy ejections are smelly. It is possible to release gas without anyone knowing about it. Unfortunately, certain foods make a real stink inside. Foods such as broccoli and cabbage release mercaptans, which smell like a cross between garlic and rotten eggs. Mercaptans have such a strong smell that they are added to domestic gas (used for heating and cooking) so you can tell if there has been a gas leak.

Some drinks, beans, dairy, and fruit can make you gassy inside.

FACT 98

You can buy underwear that filters out bad smells released by your bottom.

Silent or violent?

If you avoid the smell, you might still be embarrassed by a noise. The gas causes vibrations in the tissue around your bottom as it exits. Some are louder than others, depending on the amount of gas and how your bottom muscles work. You can try to squeeze tight, but once you relax, it will come out—possibly while you sleep. That's why bedrooms can be so smelly!

Up or down

So, what's the difference between a burp and a bottom burp? When you burp, gas from your stomach goes up and out through your mouth. However, gas from the intestines heads down and out. Pardon you!

121

A KIDNEY IS THE SIZE OF A COMPUTER MOUSE

Most people have two kidneys, each the size of a mouse. They are below the bottom ribs, at the back of your body. They filter your blood and make urine to remove all sorts of waste.

ALL THE BLOOD IN THE BODY FLOWS THROUGH THE KIDNEYS IN JUST FIVE MINUTES.

Blood filters

After your digestive system has taken the goodness it needs from your food, it is left with waste products. These are carried in your bloodstream, and pass through the kidneys to be taken out and disposed of. Each kidney contains about a million tiny filtering units called nephrons so it can do its job effectively.

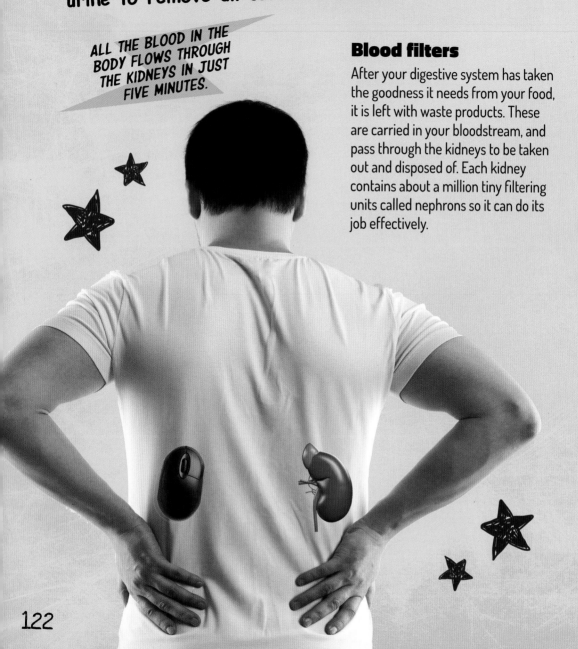

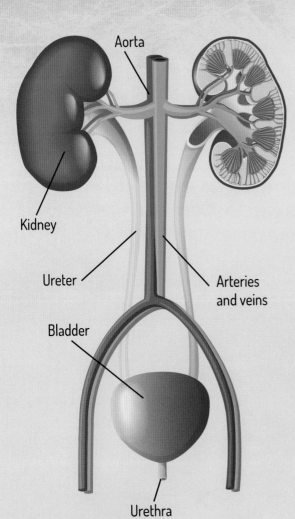

Aorta

Kidney

Ureter

Bladder

Arteries
and veins

Urethra

Pushing on through

Each kidney is connected to the bladder with tubes called ureters. Urine from the kidneys is pushed along these tubes in waves, similar to those used in digestion. This enables your body to work even if it is lying down; how many times have you woken in the night and been aware that you need to pee?

Holding on

Passing out waste can use a lot of water. Your body needs to stay well hydrated, but your kidneys have it all under control. If you haven't drunk enough, or have sweated out a lot of moisture, then the kidneys make less urine to keep the levels of fluid well balanced.

IT IS POSSIBLE TO LIVE WITH JUST ONE WORKING KIDNEY.

Organ swap

A patient with kidney failure can receive a transplant from a donor, so each has a single healthy kidney. The first successful transplant was carried out in 1954 between identical twins. Studies show that a single kidney grows faster and larger, to do the work of two kidneys.

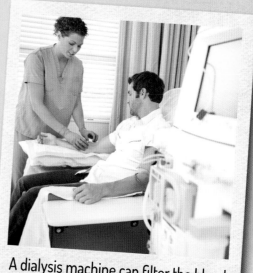

A dialysis machine can filter the blood if the kidneys aren't working properly.

FREEZING COLD MAKES YOU WANT TO PEE!

Your body tries to protect itself in very cold conditions. Your blood pressure changes to stop its extremities getting cold, and it increases the amount of urine you produce.

Under pressure

Scientists have only recently understood why you need the bathroom more when it is cold. It is a phenomenon known as cold diuresis. As the temperature drops, the blood vessels get thinner to stop as much blood passing near the surface of the skin. This increases the blood pressure, so the kidneys react by taking out more water and passing it into the bladder. The result? You need to pee, now!

THE BLADDER RECEIVES URINE FROM THE KIDNEYS EVERY 10 TO 15 SECONDS.

Time to go

Under normal circumstances, you can hold on for quite some time before you run to the bathroom. Urine is stored anywhere between one and eight hours. The bladder usually sends signals to the brain when it is half full, and most people can wait a while, even after the brain knows you've got to go.

Waiting too long to relieve yourself can weaken the bladder muscles.

See the signs

The amount of water in your urine affects how it looks and smells. Pale yellow urine is a sign of a healthy, hydrated system. If you see that it is a much darker yellow, turning to honey-brown, with a stronger smell, you should drink more water immediately.

What has happened?!

Sometimes, the things you eat can change the smell of your urine. Asparagus can have an instant effect and creates a distinctive, wet-plant kind of scent. Garlic, coffee, and puffed wheat cereals can also make urine smell different. Strangely, not everyone produces the scent—and not everyone can smell it.

CHOCOLATE MAKES YOU HAPPY!

Your body can produce special chemicals, called endorphins, to act as a painkiller. They can also make you happy, and they are released by all sorts of food, from chocolate and strawberries to Brazil nuts and spicy foods.

Extreme emotions

Endorphins are neurotransmitters: chemical messengers that pass signals around your body. They are made when you feel afraid, stressed, or in pain, and they block the brain's nerve signals. A woman's body releases endorphins during childbirth to help her through the experience. Endorphins are produced in the pituitary gland, the spinal cord, and some sections of the brain, and they can make you feel good, as well as shutting out pain.

FRESH AIR AND SUNLIGHT CAN ALSO IMPROVE YOUR MOOD.

Playing an instrument makes more endorphins than listening to music.

Happy days

Chocolate and strawberries aren't the only foods that trigger endorphins. Other "happy" foods include avocados, pasta, and hot peppers. Some smells stimulate endorphins, so try sniffing vanilla or lavender. Studies have also shown that laughing, music, and exercise boosts these feel-good chemicals.

Step outside

Serotonin is another of the body's neurotransmitters that works wonders. It balances your mood, helps you sleep, and helps wounds to heal. Some is made in your intestines and aids your digestive system. It is produced by exercise, exposure to bright light, and foods such as nuts, cheese, and red meat.

Double boost

A neurotransmitter called dopamine helps to regulate your emotional responses by controlling the brain's reward and pleasure areas. Oxytocin is another chemical, sometimes called the "cuddle hormone," that improves social interaction, trust, and healthy relationships. Simply sharing a hug can lift your oxytocin levels.

STUDIES SUGGEST THAT STROKING AND CUDDLING PETS INCREASES OXYTOCIN IN YOUR BODY.

Index